SAN FRANCISCO

0   500 m
0   500 yds

1 ★ ↑ Alcatraz

STREET POINT
BAY STREET

THE EMBA...

Pioneer Park

NORTH BEACH

6 Coit Tower

Washington Square

na Coolbrith Park

COLUMBUS AVENUE

TELEGRAPH HILL

9 Exploratorium

NORTHEAST WATERFRONT HISTORIC DISTRICT

BROADWAY STREET

Walton Park

CHINATOWN Transamerica Pyramid

Ferry Building & the Embarcadero

WASHINGTON STREET

able Car Museum **2**

Chinese Historical Society of America

23

10

FINANCIAL DISTRICT

OB HILL **4**

rrace edral **14**

Huntington Park

CALIFORNIA STREET

STREET

STEUART STREET

Oakland Museum of California 20 ★
UC Berkeley Campus 24 ★

MONTGOMERY STREET

Union Square

MARKET STREET

FREMONT STREET

2ND STREET

TRANSBAY TEMPORARY TERMINAL

STREET

80

GEARY STREET

Contemporary Jewish Museum **7**

MISSION STREET

22 **San Francisco Museum of Modern Art**

UPPER LEVEL

SOUTH BEACH

OIN

25

Yerba Buena Gardens

5TH STREET

4TH STREET

STREET

2ND STREET

SOUTH OF MARKET

HOWARD STREET

HARRISON STREET

South Park

South Beach Harbor Park

6TH STREET

7TH STREET

8TH STREET

South of Market Park

STREET

BRYANT STREET

4TH STREET

STREET

SAN FRANCISCO CALTRAIN STATION

China Basin Park

ISSION STREET

STREET

STREET

HARRISON STREET

7TH STREET

BRANNAN STREET

KING STREET

MISSION BAY

Mission Bay Commons

KYWAY (ELEVATED)

(P)   (Q)   (R)   (S)

CITYPACK GUIDE TO
San Francisco

Contents

KEY TO SYMBOLS

- Map reference to the accompanying pull-out map
- ⊠ Address
- ☎ Telephone number
- ◎ Opening/closing times
- 🍽 Restaurant or café
- 🚉 Nearest rail station
- Ⓜ Nearest subway (BART) station
- 🚌 Nearest bus route

- 🛳 Nearest riverboat or ferry stop
- ♿ Facilities for visitors with disabilities
- 🛈 Tourist information
- ❓ Other practical information
- 💵 Admission charges: Expensive (over $13), Moderate ($7–$13) and Inexpensive (under $7)
- ▷ Further information

Introducing San Francisco

 Since the Gold Rush transformed San Francisco from a hamlet into a city in the 1850s, it has been different from other cities. An anything-goes atmosphere of the early days forged a lasting mood of tolerance and a welcoming attitude toward change.

Home to a multitude of races, religions and cultures, San Francisco is intensely cosmopolitan. The diverse population has fueled the personality of the city and its multicultural draws: the varied dining scene; museums and galleries celebrating the experiences and contributions of Asians, Africans, Jews and many other groups; and neighborhoods like Chinatown and the Latino Mission District that show the vitality of these communities today.

San Francisco has frequently set the nation's cultural and social pace, and it continues to do so. It witnessed the birth of the 1950s Beat Generation, of the hippie era in the 1960s, and of the gay and lesbian liberation movement in the 1970s. Through the 1990s, its multimedia and internet companies set the pace for the global information revolution. Today, companies like Google, Facebook and Apple are ensuring that the area continues to lead the charge in the next wave of technological advances. On environmental issues, San Francisco is leading the charge as well. It now reuses 80 percent of its waste and is officially known as one of the greenest cities in the US.

Despite its importance on the national and international stage, San Francisco is small by big-city standards, housing about 820,000 people on a peninsula that is not only scenically spectacular but also prevents sprawl. The area divides into neighborhoods linked by public transportation and many are easy to walk between and through, and are well within reach of downtown, the business hub, and tourist-heavy Fisherman's Wharf.

It's easy to understand why this city is one of the best loved in the US. As the *San Francisco Chronicle* columnist Herb Caen once said, "One day if I do go to heaven, I'll look around and say, 'It ain't bad, but it ain't San Francisco.'"

FACTS AND FIGURES

- In the event of another Bay Area earthquake like the ones in 1906 and 1989, the Golden Gate Bridge is designed to sway 27.7ft (8.4m).
- San Francisco's steepest streets, Filbert and 22nd streets, have a 31.5 percent gradient.
- The city's iconic cable cars are the only National Historic Landmarks that travel.

WHAT'S IN A NAME

In 1835 San Francisco was a growing settlement called Yerba Buena (Spanish for "good herb"), but after the United States laid claim to California during the Mexican-American War, the territory was renamed San Francisco. The start of the Gold Rush followed in 1848 and 1849, transforming the city and giving a future football team its name.

CAUGHT ON FILM

Scenic hills and views make the city an enticing place as a backdrop for films (▷ 171). Classic movies filmed here include *Vertigo* (1958), *The Maltese Falcon* (1941), *The Caine Mutiny* (1954) and *The Graduate* (1967). More recently, *The Pursuit of Happyness* (2006) and *The Rock* (1996) were shot in San Francisco.

EMPEROR NORTON

Wearing epaulettes and a cockaded hat, eccentric businessman Joshua Norton proclaimed himself "Emperor of the United States and Protector of Mexico" in 1856. He was effectively accepted as such in San Francisco, though his antics were dismissed by the US government. On his death in 1880, the city's flags flew at half-mast.

Focus On Outdoor Activities

There's a good reason why San Francisco is regularly ranked among the top fittest cities in the US. Folks in this town get up early to run, bike and swim—not to mention playing golf, tennis and other sports. The area is also blessed with unique outdoor fitness options, including urban stairway walks, stunning Marin trails and free tennis courts.

Hiking and Bicycling
San Francisco and Marin County may be the Holy Grail for hiking and bicycling enthusiasts. The flat path along the Marina Green and Crissy Field (▷ 37) is popular with bicyclists, runners and casual walkers. Many bicyclists then ride across the Golden Gate Bridge and continue into Marin—views from the Coastal/Matt Davis trail in Mount Tamalpais State Park are incredible. Golden Gate Park (▷ 38–39), Angel Island (▷ 75) and many swaths of the Golden Gate National Recreation Area (▷ 36–37) also offer excellent trails to accommodate various fitness levels. Bicycle rental shops are easy to find, especially near Fisherman's Wharf.

Stairway Walks
You don't need to leave the city to go on a hike. With more than 40 hills and 300 stairways, San Francisco offers urban hikes for the energetic traveler. The stairs are usually made of concrete in urban areas and wood elsewhere. Memorable stairway walks include the Filbert Steps, which start near Coit Tower and end in Levi Plaza; the Lyon Stairs, popular with boot camps on weekday mornings (Lyon between Broadway and Green); and scenic Land's End, part of the Golden Gate National Recreation Area (visit www.parkscon-servancy.org/visit/park-sites/lands-end.html for additional information). The famous Dipsea Race in Mill Valley (in Marin) includes stairs.

Clockwise from top: Windsurfers in front of the Golden Gate Bridge; climbing the Filbert Steps, near Coit Tower; San Francisco has more than 150 public tennis courts;

Water Sports

Intrepid surfers brave the chilly waters of Ocean Beach, a popular Bay Area surfing spot. Wearing a wetsuit is a must, and take precautions—this beach is known for strong currents. To rent a wetsuit or surfboard near Ocean Beach, try Aqua Surf Shop (2830 Sloat Boulevard; tel 415/242–9283). In Golden Gate Park, visit Stow Lake Bike & Boat Rentals (50 Stow Lake Drive; tel 415/386–2531) to rent four-person rowboats or paddleboats. Across the Golden Gate Bridge in Sausalito, Sea Trek Sausalito (▷ 77) is the place to go for kayak rentals and guided trips on the water. The Bay Area also has a number of harbors and plenty of sailing and windsurfing opportunities.

Golf and Tennis

While the majority of the state's 1,000 or more golf courses are in Southern California, the Bay Area has its fair share. Popular public courses include the Presidio Golf Course (tel 415/561–GOLF; www.presidiogolf.com) and Lincoln Park Golf Club (tel 415/221–9911; sfpublicgolf.com/lincolnpark). San Francisco also has more than 150 public tennis courts, around 130 of which can be used free of charge (visit www.sftenniscourts.com).

Spectator Sports

Professional sports teams in the Bay Area include the San Francisco Giants (tel 415/972–2000; http://sanfrancisco.giants.mlb.com) and the East Bay's Oakland A's (tel 510/638–4627; http://oakland.athletics.mlb.com), both part of Major League Baseball; Oakland's Golden State Warriors (tel 510/986–2200; www.nba.com/warriors), part of the National Basketball Association; and two teams from the National Football League—the Oakland Raiders (tel 510/864–5000; www.raiders.com) and the San Francisco 49ers (tel 415/656–4900; www.49ers.com).

fans cheer their heroes at the San Francisco Giants victory parade, in 2010; a bicyclist in Marin County admires the Golden Gate Bridge; surfing the waves

Top Tips For...

These great suggestions will help you tailor your ideal visit to San Francisco, no matter how you choose to spend your time.

...Late-Night Dining
Eat in the Western Addition at **NoPa** (▷ 147) or **Tsunami** (▷ 149).
Brave the gritty Tenderloin neighborhood for Indian fare at **Shalimar** (▷ 148).
Nibble on small plates at **Alembic** (▷ 132) in the Upper Haight.

...Learning About Different Cultures
Take a tour of the **Mission District Murals** (▷ 71–72).
Learn about the African diaspora at **MoAD** (▷ 72).
Walk around the neighborhoods of **Japantown** (▷ 46–47) and **Chinatown** (▷ 67).
Visit the **Contemporary Jewish Museum** (▷ 26–27).

...Vintage or Funky Finds
Pay a visit to **Ver Unica** (▷ 126–127) in Hayes Valley.
Peruse Haight Street in **Haight–Ashbury** (▷ 42–43, 121) for the best wacky, vintage clothes outlets.
Discover secondhand designer clothes at **Cris** (▷ 123).
Head over to the **Mission District** (▷ 71–72, 121) to shop, where you will find a range of funky designs.

...Outdoor Activities
Boat across Stow Lake in **Golden Gate Park** (▷ 38–39).
Bike to **Sausalito** (▷ 77) via the **Golden Gate Bridge** (▷ 34–35).
Hike around **Angel Island** (▷ 75).
Surf at Ocean Beach in the **Golden Gate National Recreation Area** (▷ 36–37).

Clockwise from top left: Colorful clothes for sale in Haight–Ashbury; walking across Golden Gate Bridge; enjoying the view at Greens restaurant; Cobb's is a

...Saving Money
Ride to the top of the observation tower (free entry) at the **de Young Museum** (▷ 28–29).
Walk along the pedestrian path of the **Golden Gate Bridge** (▷ 34–35).
Enjoy a burrito at **Taqueria Cancun** in the **Mission** (▷ 149).
Get in free at the city's cathedrals, **Grace** (▷ 40–41) and **St. Mary's** (▷ 73).

...Entertaining Your Children
Jump on a **cable car** (▷ 167) .
Visit the Tactile Dome at the **Exploratorium** (▷ 30–31).
Meet the animals at the **San Francisco Zoo** (▷ 75).
Take the ferry over to **Alcatraz** for a fun history lesson (▷ 14–15).

...Dining with a View
Enjoy vegetarian food and bay views at **Greens** (▷ 145).
Admire the Bay Bridge while dining at **Boulevard** (▷ 143).
Watch the cable car chug by at **Zarzuela** (▷ 149).
Have a pisco sour and ceviche along the **Embarcadero** (▷ 32–33).

...Hearty Laughs
See an improv show at **BATS** (▷ 133), in Fort Mason.
Check out the stand-up comedians at **Punch Line** comedy club (▷ 136).
See who's topping the bill at **Cobb's** (▷ 134).
View an exhibition at the **Cartoon Art Museum** (▷ 66–67).

...Specialty Books and Magazines
Learn about the Beat Generation at **City Lights** (▷ 123).
Find indie magazines at **Needles & Pens** (▷ 126).

great place for comedy; books line the shelves at City Lights; boating on Stow Lake, in Golden Gate Park

Timeline

1769 The Spanish discover San Francisco Bay.

1821 Mexico takes California from Spain.

1846 The United States takes control of California by force from Mexico.

1848–49 The California Gold Rush begins. San Francisco's population soars from only 812 to 20,000 as the city becomes the commercial center for miners.

GAY PROTEST

In 1977 Harvey Milk became the nation's first openly gay male to be elected to public office. The following year, Milk and Mayor George Moscone were assassinated at City Hall by a former city politician, Dan White. The lightweight five-year prison sentence bestowed on White prompted the White Night Riots; predominantly gay demonstrators marched on City Hall, causing $1 million worth of damage. The 2008 film *Milk* tells Harvey Milk's story (▷ 171).

1873 The first cable car runs along Clay Street.

1906 San Francisco is ruined by earthquake and fire.

1915 The Panama Pacific International Exposition symbolizes the city's recovery from the earthquake.

1937 The Golden Gate Bridge is completed.

1941 US entry into World War II stimulates war industries and brings an influx of military and civilian personnel to the city. Employment in the shipyards increases from 4,000 to 260,000.

1945 50 countries sign the United Nations charter in the SF Opera House.

1964 Students at Berkeley form the non-violent Free Speech Movement and instigate the first of many campus revolts in the country.

A cable car in the 1880s

A vast crack in one of the city's roads, caused by the 1906 earthquake

THE GREAT EARTHQUAKE

Striking at 5.12am on April 18, 1906, the earthquake measured 7.9 on the Richter scale but caused relatively minor damage. By rupturing gas and water mains, however, it caused fires to break out and burn uncontrolled for three days. Over 3,000 acres (1,215ha) of San Francisco was devastated, 250,000 of the city's 400,000 inhabitants were made homeless and 300 died (later reports suggest as many as 3,000 perished). The quake was a forceful reminder of the area's geological instability; the recovery highlighted San Francisco's regenerative powers, symbolized by the city's official emblem, the phoenix.

1966 The militant African-American group the Black Panthers forms in Oakland.

1967 The "Summer of Love": Young people arrive from across the US and Haight–Ashbury's hippie population grows to 75,000.

1989 The Loma Prieta earthquake (7.1 on the Richter scale) kills 67 people and closes the Bay Bridge for a month.

1995 Willie Brown becomes the city's first black mayor.

1996 San Francisco becomes the first local government to sue the tobacco industry.

1998 It becomes illegal to smoke in public indoor spaces.

1999 The $3.3 billion injected into San Francisco-based dotcom companies reshapes the city's economic base.

2004 Much publicized same-sex weddings take place at City Hall as 1,600 gay couples apply for licenses.

2007 San Francisco Representative Nancy Pelosi becomes the first female—and the first Californian—Speaker of the US House of Representatives.

2010 San Francisco's Major League Baseball team, the Giants, wins the World Series for the first time since moving from New York City in 1958.

2013 After a nine-year legal and political battle, gays and lesbians in California win the right to marry.

A Haight–Ashbury mural

"BEATNIKS"

The 1957 publication of Allen Ginsberg's poem *Howl* by North Beach bookstore-publisher City Lights (▷ 123) made the area a prime destination for what long-time *San Francisco Chronicle* columnist Herb Caen labeled "beatniks."

Top 25

This section contains the must-see Top 25 sights and experiences in San Francisco. They are listed alphabetically, and numbered so you can locate them on the inside front cover map.

TOP 25

DID YOU KNOW?

● Named: Isla de los Alcatraces (Island of Pelicans), 1775
● Island size: 22 acres (9ha)
● Number of prisoners: 1,545
● Number of cells: 378

TIPS

● There is no food service on the island, so consider a snack on the ferry ride over.
● The evening tour is more expensive than the day tours.

Easily viewed from any high point in the city, Alcatraz is as much a part of San Francisco as the Golden Gate Bridge or cable cars. The former prison sits on Alcatraz Island in San Francisco Bay and is the city's most chilling sight.

No escape Alcatraz became the country's most feared place of incarceration from 1934, after the federal government took control of the island. It was turned into a top-security penitentiary for "incorrigible" criminals (those deemed beyond salvation and considered too dangerous to be held at conventional jails). There was one guard for every three inmates, work was a privilege that had to be earned through good behavior, and prisoners who did escape faced the prospect of crossing the freezing, swiftly

Alcatraz was a grim place of incarceration from 1934 until 1963; today visitors can tour the former prison and get a glimpse of what life was like for the inmates

moving waters of the bay (regarded as unswimmable) to freedom. Known escape attempts number 36 inmates in 14 separate attempts; five escapees are unaccounted for.

Moody viewing The former cells, mess hall, hospital and exercise yard are all open for viewing, and an audio tour with a terse commentary by former Alcatraz guards and inmates makes an excellent atmospheric accompaniment. The costs and difficulties of running an island prison, and public disquiet at the severity of the regime, contributed to Alcatraz's closure in 1963. A small museum traces the broader history of the island, which was claimed and occupied by Native Americans in 1969 for 19 months under a treaty of 1868 that granted them rights to "unused government land."

THE BASICS

www.nps.gov/alc
➕ Off map at Q1
✉ San Francisco Bay
☎ 415/981–7625
🕐 Daily, according to first and last ferries
🚢 Alcatraz Cruises from Pier 33, Fisherman's Wharf
♿ Few
💲 Expensive. Advance reservations advised in summer; buy tickets online at www.alcatrazcruises.com

The ring of the cable-car bell provides a constant reminder that you are in San Francisco, probably the only city in the world where a relatively inefficient form of public transportation is adored by the entire population.

Inspired Legend has it that a horse, slipping while trying to drag its load up a San Franciscan hill, inspired Andrew Smith Hallidie to invent the cable car. Wire rope had previously been used as a means of transporting materials in gold mines, but Hallidie was the first to develop the idea as a means of moving people. Damage caused by the 1906 earthquake and fire, and the subsequent rise of motorized transportation, soon rendered cable cars obsolete. Pressure from San Franciscans led the

Find out how this much-loved form of city transportation works at the Cable Car Museum

federal government to award National Historic Landmark status to cable cars in 1964, however, and a provision in the city's charter ensures preservation of the remaining lines.

Simple but effective The museum's intriguing memorabilia, including the first cable car, tell the story of the system's development. The clever engineering principle that keeps the cars running is also revealed: Each one is pulled by an underground cable that never stops moving. The "gripman" on each car uses a lever to connect or disconnect the car to or from the cable through a slot in the road. The whirring sound, audible as you enter the museum, is the noise made by the steel cable as it is pulled over winding wheels that are 14ft (4.5m) wide, a process visible in the museum's lower level.

THE BASICS

www.cablecarmuseum.org

➕ P4

✉ 1201 Mason Street

☎ 415/474-1887

🕐 Apr–Sep daily 10–6; Oct–Mar 10–5

🚌 1, 3, 12, 45; Powell–Mason or Powell–Hyde cable car

♿ Good

💲 Free

★3 California Academy of Sciences

● Morrison Planetarium
● The Living Roof
● The Academy Café and the fancier Moss Room, both helmed by first-rate chefs

TIP

● On Thursday evenings, from 6pm to 10pm, the museum hosts a nightlife event for adults, who are invited to drink, dance and take in the exhibits.

One of the most popular attractions in the Bay Area has a huge variety of changing programmes and activities. The newest addition shelters a rainforest dome, planetarium, aquarium and natural history museum under its living roof. The building, designed by Renzo Piano, has gained the highest award for sustainability.

The sky The all-digital, state-of-the-art Morrison Planetarium is the biggest draw at the museum. Popular shows about the stars and planets happen every half hour during the week, and every 45 minutes on weekends. There is no extra cost, but visitors need a separate ticket, which is handed out on a first-come, first-served basis. It's advisable to get your tickets before you start exploring the museum.

A rainforest, planetarium and aquarium are among the attractions at the California Academy of Sciences

Land and sea Near the Planetarium on the main floor is the Kimball Natural History Museum and the hall of dioramas. The exhibits cover topics like evolution on remote islands, how climate change is affecting California's natural habitat and the diverse ecosystems of Africa. You can also peek through windows to see Academy scientists doing their research. Downstairs is the Steinhart Aquarium, with 38,000 live animals across 900 species. Be warned that the space can feel a bit cramped.

The forest The museum also has a rainforest—within a glass dome—that houses an array of tropical plants and 1,600 animals, from a cave of bats to reptiles and butterflies. The temperature here is 82°F to 85°F (28°C to 29°C), plus 75 percent humidity.

THE BASICS

www.calacademy.org

🔢 G7

✉ 55 Music Concourse Drive, Golden Gate Park

☎ 415/379–8000

🕐 Mon–Sat 9.30–5, Sun 11–5

🚌 5, 44, N–Judah

♿ Good

💰 Expensive

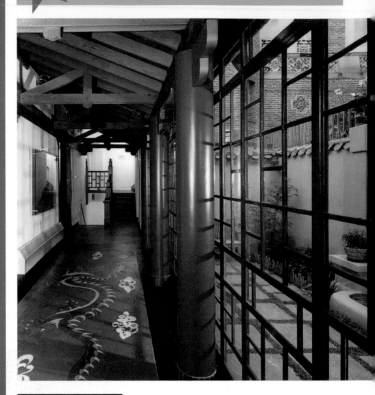

The Chinese have been present for longer, and in much greater numbers, than any other non-Anglo ethnic group in San Francisco, greatly contributing to the city's multicultural character.

Early days The Chinese arrived in California in force during the Gold Rush, but met racial hostility and the foreign miners' tax. They were unjustly blamed for the economic depression that followed the gold boom and were eventually forced into "Chinatown" communities, the largest being in San Francisco. Chinatown became populated almost exclusively by males who wore traditional dress and tied their hair in braids. Developing into the city's most densely populated district, Chinatown was composed of wooden buildings divided by slender alleyways

Learn about the history and culture of the Chinese-American community at the Chinese Historical Society of America

where, denied the comforts of traditional family life, many Chinese men gambled, smoked opium, joined the secret Chinese-American societies known as tongs and visited prostitutes to alleviate the boredom—activities that added to the area's mystique.

Recent times Not until the founding of the Chinese Republic in 1911 were the Chinese able to adopt Western ideas and modes of dress. By the 1920s, Chinatown's restaurants and shops were becoming tourist attractions and the Chinese, expanded in numbers through the easing of immigration restrictions, steadily became an accepted part of life. This tiny museum tells the story of the Chinese in California, with exhibits ranging from an antique silver pagoda to gold-mining paraphernalia.

THE BASICS

www.chsa.org

🚻 P4

✉ 965 Clay Street

☎ 415/391–1188

🕐 Tue–Fri 12–5, Sat 11–4

🚌 1, 30; Powell–Hyde cable car

♿ Few

🎟 Inexpensive; free 1st Thu of month

TOP 25

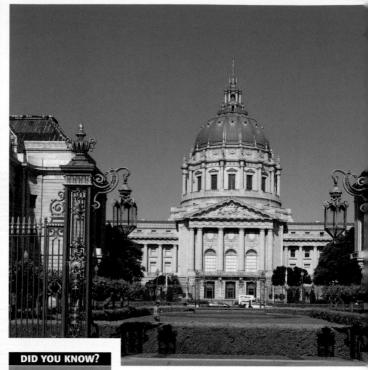

The crowning glory of the Civic Center, City Hall is a beaux-arts masterpiece with a dome that can be seen from many points around San Francisco. Its aesthetic appeal makes it seem an entirely fitting place from which to conduct San Francisco day-to-day administrative affairs.

A symbol City Hall's immense rotunda is topped by a black-and-gold copper dome (possibly modeled on St. Peter's, in Rome) visible across much of the city. This intricate and inspiring building at the heart of San Francisco was completed in 1915, and arose from the drawing boards of architects Arthur Brown and John Bakewell (both of whom studied at the École des Beaux-Arts in Paris). In San Francisco, the authorities were eager for a building to

City Hall was commissioned to show San Francisco's superiority over rival Los Angeles; its architects used the French baroque style to great effect

symbolize San Francisco's superiority over fast-growing Los Angeles. It was Brown and Bakewell's plan—based on the French baroque style, making free use of marble and with hardly a square inch left bare of some form of decoration—that won the day.

Impressive interior Go inside and climb the grand staircase, which is lined by ornate wrought-iron banisters and illuminated by freestanding and hanging lamps, and wander around the landings where porticoes and arches, topped by neoclassical sculptured guardians, give access to the upper levels. With the removal of the county courts, the building gained space as well as strength after a four-year, $300-million structural refit completed in 1999.

THE BASICS

www.sfgsa.org (then enter keyword "City Hall")

➕ N6

✉ 1 Dr. Carlton B. Goodlett Place

☎ 415/554–4000

🕐 Mon–Fri 8–8

🚇 Civic Center or Van Ness

🚌 5, 10, 21, 47, 49

♿ Good

💷 Free

❓ Tours: Mon–Fri 10, 12, 2

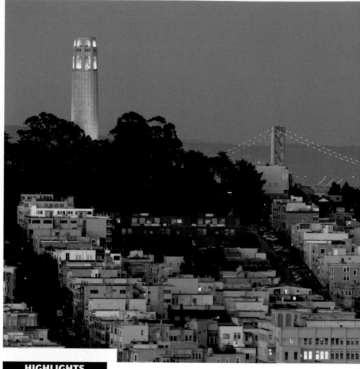

HIGHLIGHTS

● Stunning views
● 19 frescoed murals
● Observation gallery

TIPS

● Parking is available but extremely limited (about 30 spots). To avoid getting stuck in a traffic jam, opt for a bit of exercise and walk up Filbert to Coit Tower.
● The continuation of Filbert is a set of charming wooden steps that lead down to Levi Plaza.

Whether from the top of the tower or from its base, the view across San Francisco Bay and a huge swath of the city is memorable, as are the murals—part of a Depression-era project to give work to artists.

History Coit Tower was built as a monument to Lillie Hitchcock Coit, a San Francisco socialite who was passionate about the fire department —she was cremated wearing a gold pin from Engine Company Number Five—and the city. She bequeathed $125,000 to San Francisco "for the purpose of adding beauty to the city which I have always loved." Construction began soon after her death in 1929, and the tower was completed in 1933 (the surrounding summit of Telegraph Hill, called Pioneer Park, was donated to the city in 1876).

Clockwise from far left: Coit Tower at dusk, with Oakland Bridge behind it; a statue of Christopher Columbus stands nearby; artists decorated the tower's walls with murals, including the orchard scene California, by Maxine Albro; another mural—Industries of California, by Ralph Stackpole

Frescoed murals In the early 1930s, artists were paid $38 per week to work on frescoed murals, which cover the walls of the tower. They were painted in the social realist style pioneered by Diego Rivera. The style was controversial, but only one fresco was censored: The phrase "Workers of the World Unite" appeared above the depiction of a surveyor and steel worker, along with other symbols and statements. That section was covered over.

The tower This fluted concrete column has a small observation gallery at the top, accessible by elevator. Reaching a height of 180ft (55m), the monument is clearly visible from many areas of the city. Official Coit Tower literature refutes the rumor that the tower was built to look like a firehouse nozzle.

THE BASICS

➕ Q2 and Q3
✉ Summit of Telegraph Hill Boulevard
☎ 415/362-0808
🕐 Daily 10–6.30
🚌 39
♿ Few
💷 Inexpensive
❓ Guided tours of the murals Wed, Sat 11am

HIGHLIGHTS

● The unusual exterior: large blue steel shapes wedged into the 1907 brick building
● Workshops, films and lectures

TIPS

● The museum is closed the first day of Passover, July 4th, the first day of Rosh Hashanah, Yom Kippur, Thanksgiving and New Year's Day.
● A number of events are aimed exclusively at teenagers.

Famed architect Daniel Libeskind designed the Contemporary Jewish Museum, redeveloping the 1907 landmark Jessie Street Power Substation. The ambitious, 63,000sq ft (5,853sq m) building extends the original Willis Polk-designed space, juxtaposing early 20th-century architecture with contemporary design.

Old and new Libeskind created a striking exterior for the museum's new home (it moved to its SoMa quarters in 2008), preserving something old and introducing something entirely modern and new. At first glance the museum, set back from Mission Street and fronted by a lovely plaza, looks like a traditional brick building—until you see the two steel shapes wedged into its side.

Clockwise from far left: The striking Koret-Taube Grand Lobby; eye-catching lighting in the Stephen and Maribelle Leavitt "Yud" Gallery; one of the vast steel shapes wedged into the brick building; a view of the museum from Mission Street

The museum's approach isn't quite traditional, either. It doesn't have a permanent collection—instead it stages temporary exhibitions relating to Jewish art, film, music and more. The museum explores a range of themes about the Jewish identity and spirit. It also features performances and education programs, including a number of activities and events for kids.

Encouraging participation Exhibits here include interactive elements whenever possible. For example, a recent exhibit was set up as a nightclub, featuring café tables with a "menu" of songs, along with iPad listening stations. In another exhibit, a professionally trained female scribe (they're usually male) spent more than a year at the museum writing out the text of the Torah in an open studio.

THE BASICS

www.thecjm.org
➕ Q5
✉ 736 Mission Street between 3rd and 4th
☎ 415/655-7800
🕐 Mon–Tue, Fri–Sun 11–5, Thu 11–8
Ⓜ Montgomery
🚌 14, 30, 45
♿ Good
👐 Moderate; free to under-18s; inexpensive Thu after 5pm

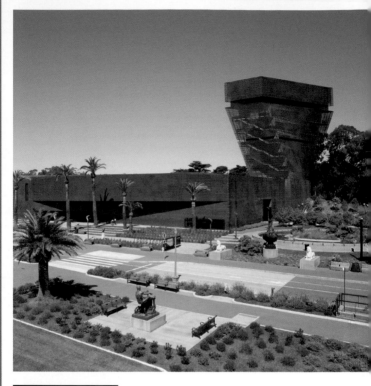

HIGHLIGHTS

● *Ocean Park: Variation #8*, Diebenkorn
● *Storm in the Rocky Mountains*, Bierstadt
● *The Ironworkers' Noontime*, Anshutz
● *Mrs. Daniel Sargent*, Copley
● *Three Machines*, Thiebaud
● *A Dinner Table at Night*, Singer Sargent
● Philadelphia High Chest of Drawers
● Observation floor of the 144ft (44m) tower

From Amish quilts to the couture of Spain's Balenciaga, this museum stocks diverse exhibits from around the world. Exemplary collections of American painting and decorative art are the main draw.

Paintings Founded in 1895 in Golden Gate Park, the de Young Museum is part of the fabric of San Francisco—even more so since it reopened in stunning new building in 2005. The museum's collection of American paintings begins with the 18th-century society portraits of John Singleton Copley and his contemporaries. From here, the museum traces the growing self-confidence of American artists and the lessening importance of European trends. By the mid-1800s, many American artists were taking inspiration from the newly settled West: The

Clockwise from far left: The de Young Museum returned to Golden Gate Park in 2005; the larger-than-life Man Observing Series II *(1984), by Viola Frey; taking a rest in the American Gallery; the museum at night*

landscapes of Albert Bierstadt and the sculpture of Frederick Remington evoke the period's celebratory mood of expansion. By contrast, Richard Diebenkorn's work is a strikingly Californian contribution to 1960s and '70s contemporary art.

Furnishings The furniture, too, reflects the US's historic shift from colony to nation as it moves from English and Dutch armchairs used in New England settlements of 1670 to a Federal-period parlor from 1805 Massachusetts. The flowing curves of the Queen Anne style were popular during the colonial period but by the time of the revolution, American craftsmen had acquired the skills and creativity to evolve a new look. Philadelphia emerged as the center of the craft, and a grand 1780 Philadelphia High Chest provides an excellent example of the period.

THE BASICS

http://deyoung.famsf.org

🚹 F7

✉ 50 Hagiwara Tea Garden Drive, Golden Gate Park

☎ 415/750–3600

🕑 Tue–Sun 9.30–5.15 (some Fri until 8.45)

🍴 Café

🚌 5, 21, 44, N–Judah

🚻 Excellent

💰 Moderate; includes the Legion of Honor (▷ 48–49) if visited on same day. Free 1st Tue of month. Observation tower free

❓ Free tours daily. Lectures, films

⭐9 Exploratorium

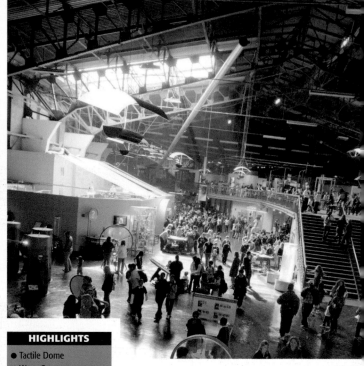

HIGHLIGHTS

- Tactile Dome
- Wave Organ
- Alien Voices
- Anti-gravity Mirror
- Bright Black
- Tune Blocks
- Distorted Room
- Shadow Box
- Soap Film Painting
- Momentum Machine

DID YOU KNOW?

● The Exploratorium has moved to a spectacular new location at Pier 15 on the Embarcadero. The new Bay Observatory has breathtaking views.

Without a doubt the best place in San Francisco to amuse young minds with low boredom thresholds, the Exploratorium, in its new waterside location, sets the pace for hands-on museums across the US.

Questions and answers Founded by Frank Oppenheimer, who worked alongside his more famous brother, Robert, on the development of the atomic bomb in the 1940s, the Exploratorium, in its brand new location, has 650 hands-on, interactive exhibits designed to illustrate and explain the fundamentals of natural science and human perception in a user-friendly environment. Helpful "explainers" stroll around the building answering questions, and new exhibits are developed in a workshop open to public view.

There are plenty of hands-on activities to amuse youngsters at the Exploratorium, including the Particle Accelerator (below) and the Liquid Mirror (bottom)

Innovative art and science Be they crackling tesla coils or coupled resonant pendulums, the permanent exhibits stand alongside a series of temporary installations. These have included "Listen: Making Sense of Sound", which enables visitors to explore how they perceive sound, and "Traits of Life," an interactive presentation on the essentials of biology.

Dark Tunnel An innovative artist-in-residence program has resulted in imaginative artworks based on scientific themes. The Exploratorium's most popular exhibit is the Tactile Dome, a dark "tunnel" designed and built by August Coppola (father of actor Nicolas Cage and brother of film director Francis Ford Coppola), from which participants can leave only by feeling their way out on their hands and knees.

THE BASICS

www.exploratorium.edu

➕ R3

✉ Pier 15 (Embarcadero at Green St)

☎ 415/528–4444; 528–4360; 528–4646; Tactile Dome reservations 415/528–4646

🕐 Tue–Sun 10–5; also Mon public hols; Thu 6–10 over 18s only

🍴 Restaurant & Café

🚌 2, 6, 9, 14, 21, 31, F

♿ Excellent

💲 Expensive; free 1st Wed of month. Entry including the Tactile Dome is more expensive

10 Ferry Building and the Embarcadero

HIGHLIGHTS

- Miette pastries
- Blue Bottle Coffee
- Cowgirl Creamery's Artisan Cheese Shop
- The Ferry Building's steel-trussed glass ceiling
- The Farmers' Market

TIP

- There's validated parking across the street at the Washington Embarcadero lot. On weekdays, valet parking is available in front of the Ferry Building.

After an extensive renovation in the 1990s, the Ferry Building and central waterfront have become center stage once again. In addition to being a transit hub, the Ferry Building also houses a large marketplace, with shops and cafés selling pastries, fresh meat, artisan cheeses, flowers and more.

Survivor's story The Ferry Building opened in 1898 and its 245ft-high (75m) clock tower was for many years the city's tallest structure. Surviving the 1906 earthquake and fire—and a plan to demolish it for safety reasons during the disaster—the slender clock tower became a symbol of San Francisco's ability to survive natural catastrophe. Ironically, another natural disaster—the 1989 Loma Prieta earthquake—actually helped the Ferry Building. The unsightly

Clockwise from far left: Looking up at Four Embarcadero; the Ferry Building's clock tower survived the 1906 earthquake; outdoor sculpture at the Embarcadero Center; the Farmers' Market; a view across the water toward the Embarcadero and Financial District; inside the Ferry Building

Embarcadero Freeway was damaged and later removed, restoring the views and the natural beauty of the waterfront.

Community hub The marketplace has a range of shops, cafés and restaurants (everything from upscale Vietnamese to burgers), while the building is also a transit hub for ferries, MUNI and BART. On Tuesday, Thursday and Saturday, the Ferry Plaza Farmers' Market sells fresh produce, flowers and more, drawing big crowds.

Stroll the Embarcadero Head south along the palm-lined Embarcadero to take in the views of the Bay Bridge and the water, and to see *Cupid's Span*, a sculpture by Claes Oldenburg and Coosje van Bruggen. It's a reference to Tony Bennett's *I Left My Heart in San Francisco*.

THE BASICS

www.ferrybuildingmarket
place.com

🚆 R4

✉ Foot of Market Street, at the Embarcadero

☎ 415/983-8030

🕐 Mon–Fri 10–6, Sat 9–6, Sun 11–5. Ferry Plaza Farmers' Market Tue, Thu 10–2, Sat 8–2

🚇 Embarcadero

🚌 2, 6, 9, 14, 21, 31, F

♿ Good

🎟 Free

11 Golden Gate Bridge

DID YOU KNOW?

● Weight of bridge, anchorages and approaches: 887,000 tons
● Actual bridge length: 6,450ft (1,966m)
● Length of central span: 4,200ft (1,280m)
● Height above water: 220ft (67m) at low tide
● Height of towers above water: 746ft (227m)
● Color: International Orange, the color most easily distinguishable in fog
● Gallons of paint used annually: 5,000 (22,727L)
● Annual vehicle crossings: more than 42 million

Named for the entrance to San Francisco Bay rather than its color, the Golden Gate Bridge must be the most recognizable, and the most beautiful, of all the bridges in the United States.

Artful engineering The bridge is a remarkable feat of artistry as well as engineering. The construction overcame the exceptional depth and strong currents of the Golden Gate, while the simple but inspired design allows it to elegantly connect the city to the hillsides of Marin County.

Loathed but then loved A bond issue of $35 million was authorized in 1930 to finance the bridge's construction, amid great antipathy from San Franciscans, many of whom feared

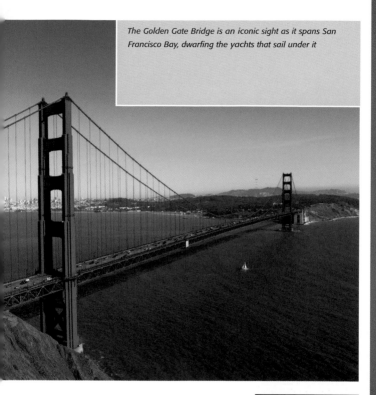

The Golden Gate Bridge is an iconic sight as it spans San Francisco Bay, dwarfing the yachts that sail under it

that it would detract from the beauty of the Golden Gate. An early design by the project's chief engineer, Joseph B. Strauss, was likened to "two grotesque steel beetles emerging from either bank." The design that was eventually adopted is thought to have been the work of Strauss's assistants. The affection the bridge enjoys has been confirmed many times over the years, and the bridge celebrated the 75th anniversary of its opening in 2012.

Fatal attraction On a more downbeat note, the Golden Gate Bridge has become a notorious spot for suicides. The first occurred three months after the bridge's opening and many more have since chosen to end it all by jumping the 220ft (67m) from the central span to the raging waters below.

THE BASICS

www.goldengatebridge.org

➕ E–F1

🕐 Open to pedestrians daily 5am–9pm (5am–6pm in winter). Open to vehicles 24 hours a day

🚌 28, 76

♿ Good at observation platform

✋ Free for pedestrians and bicyclists. Inexpensive toll for city-bound drivers

12 Golden Gate National Recreation Area

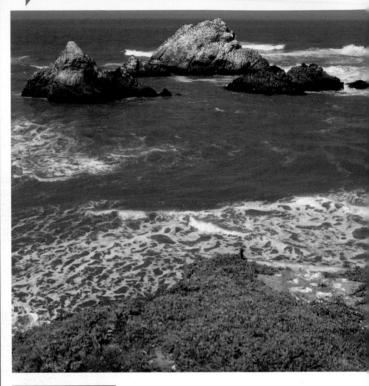

HIGHLIGHTS

- Coastal trail
- China Beach
- Baker Beach
- Fort Point (▷ 69)
- Seal Rocks
- Fort Funston
- Marin Headlands
- Crissy Field
- Ocean Beach
- Golden Gate Promenade

TIP

- Baker Beach is the perfect spot for a rest.

An enormous swath of mostly undeveloped land lying within the city and extending northward across the Golden Gate Bridge, the Golden Gate National Recreation Area is a good reminder of how open most of California is.

Creation From the cliffs of Fort Funston in the south to the hills of Marin County in the north, the Golden Gate National Recreation Area bestows federal protection on a long chunk of San Francisco's coastline. The area's 75,500 acres (30,553ha), which lie in separate pockets and often lack clearly marked boundaries, were created in 1972 by the amalgamation of city parks, private land and former military-owned areas. Abandoned fortifications include a Civil War fort (Fort Point, ▷ 69, located beneath the

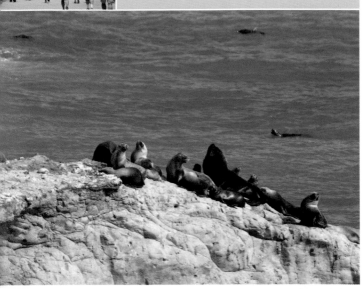

Clockwise from far left: White foaming surf hits Seal Rocks; walkers, runners and bicyclists enjoy views of the Golden Gate Bridge at Crissy Field; you may be lucky enough to spot sea lions at Seal Rocks

Golden Gate Bridge) and a massive World War II cannon at Baker Beach.

Exploration Much of Golden Gate NRA is best explored on foot. Start at the Cliff House, close to the sea lion-frequented Seal Rocks. Walk the coastal trail that weaves through the coarsely vegetated hillsides, which rise steeply above the tiny beach of Lands End and the forbidding waters of the Golden Gate. All vestiges of the city are hidden until the appearance of the Golden Gate Bridge. This route also brings views of China Beach, named for the Chinese fishermen of the Gold Rush era who lived in shacks beside it. China Beach is one of the few San Francisco beaches safe for swimming. Crissy Field, formerly a military airfield, has been restored to tidal marsh and beaches.

THE BASICS

www.nps.gov/goga

➕ E3, G2

ℹ️ 415/561–4700

🕐 Daylight hours only recommended

🍴 Beach Hut Café, 1199 East Beach; daily 9–5 (also has tourist leaflets)

🚌 5, 18, 19, 28, 29, 30, 31, 38, 48, 76 travel to various parts of the GGNRA

♿ Range from none to excellent according to location

💲 Free

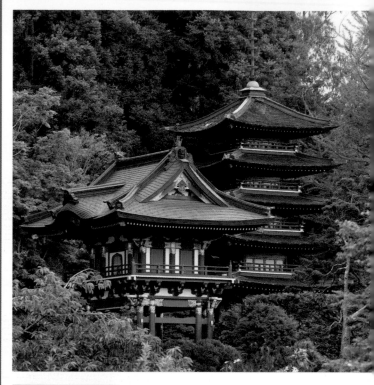

HIGHLIGHTS

● Conservatory of Flowers
● Japanese Tea Garden
● Windmills
● Stow Lake
● California Academy of Sciences

TIP

● If you're traveling with children, try a boat ride on Stow Lake (☎ 415/752-0347) or a ride on the carousel, which was at the 1939 World's Fair on Treasure Island.

Once a desolate stretch of sand dunes, Golden Gate Park is now a massive slab of greenery holding several museums. It's also a stage from which San Francisco, and its jogging, kite-flying, roller-skating population, presents its playful side to the world.

Acres of fun Some 3.5 miles (5.6km) long and half a mile (1km) wide, Golden Gate Park is one of the world's largest urban parks. Within its 1,000 acres (405ha) is the de Young Museum (▷ 28–29), the California Academy of Sciences (▷ 18–19) and many other major attractions, plus a polo field, golf course, archery range, botanical garden, lakes, waterfalls, two windmills and a bison paddock. Yet there is still sufficient space to become hopelessly lost amid tree-shrouded lanes and footpaths.

Clockwise from far left: Pagodas in the Japanese Tea Garden; strolling in the Strybing Arboretum; vividly colored callistemon (bottlebrush) flowers; rowing on Stow Lake; the Dutch Windmill in the Queen Wilhelmina Tulip Garden

On foot The park is too large to cover entirely on foot but the eastern half is fine for strolling. Here you'll find the redstone McLaren Lodge, former office of the park's creator and now an information center (maps are essential), and the AIDS Memorial Grove, a 7.5 acre (3ha) wooded grove and scene of private services following the loss of a loved one to AIDS. Nearby is the Conservatory of Flowers (▷ 68), with its tropical vegetation, and the Japanese Tea Garden (▷ 70–71), with azaleas, cherry trees and a carp-filled pond. West of the Tea Garden a road encircles Stow Lake, at the center of which Strawberry Hill rises to a 400ft (122m) summit. South of the Tea Garden is the San Francisco Botanical Garden at Strybing Arboretum (▷ 74), which offers free guided walks daily at 1.30 (also 10.30 on weekends).

THE BASICS

www.golden-gate-park.com

✚ F7

✉ Bordered by Great Highway, Lincoln Way, Fulton and Stanyan streets

☎ 415/831–2700

🕐 Daylight hours only recommended

🍴 Tea at Japanese Tea Garden; cafés at de Young Museum and California Academy of Sciences

🚌 5, 18, 21, 28, 29, 33, 44, 71, N–Judah

♿ Good

💲 Park free

ℹ Park Visitor Center: Beach Chalet, 1000 Great Highway (at western end of park, just south of Fulton Street), tel 415/386–8439; Mon–Fri 9–4

HIGHLIGHTS

● Ghiberti doors
● Chapel of Grace
● Stained-glass windows
● Rose window
● Indoor and outdoor labyrinths
● Gobelin tapestry

DID YOU KNOW?

● Huntington Park, facing the cathedral, is named for railroad baron Collis P. Huntington.

It would be nice to think that Grace Cathedral, located as it is on the site of a former robber-baron's Nob Hill mansion, provides some spiritual atonement for the materialist excesses that characterize the neighborhood.

Slow building When the mansion of railroad boss Charles Crocker was destroyed by the fire that followed San Francisco's 1906 earthquake, the Crocker family donated the land to the Episcopalian church. Although the cathedral's cornerstone was laid in 1910, construction did not begin until 1928, and further delays (due partly to the Depression) resulted in Grace Cathedral's consecration being postponed until 1964. Described by its main architect, Lewis P. Hobart, as "a truly American cathedral," the

Highlights of Grace Cathedral include the stained-glass windows (left and far left) and the gilded bronze doors (bottom), from the same cast as the Gates of Paradise doors in Florence's Baptistery

cathedral is in fact neo-Gothic in style, partly modeled on Notre-Dame in Paris.

Through the doors The most impressive part of the exterior is a pair of gilded bronze doors from the Lorenzo Ghiberti cast that was used for the Gates of Paradise doors of the Baptistery in Florence. Inside, a 15th-century French altar-piece and an exquisite Flemish reredos can be seen in the Chapel of Grace, while the stained-glass windows depict biblical scenes and diverse achievers such as Albert Einstein and Henry Ford. The cathedral has, controversially, frequently hosted radical figures invited to speak from its pulpit. There are two labyrinths at the cathedral, one outdoors and one indoors. Both are modeled after the famous labyrinth at Chartres Cathedral in France.

THE BASICS

www.gracecathedral.org

✚ P4

✉ 1100 California Street at Taylor Street

☎ 415/749–6300

🕐 Sun–Fri 7–6, Sat 8–6

🚌 1; California Street cable car

♿ Good

❓ 90-minute "grand tours" for over 10s; must be booked in advance online; expensive—check the website for details

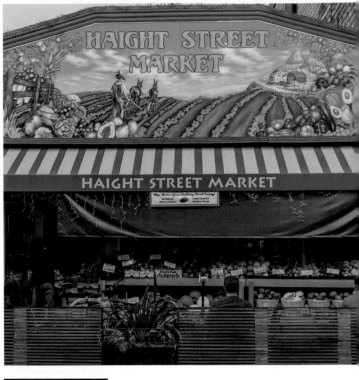

This neighborhood of San Francisco is known the world over for being the epicenter of the social earthquake that was the 1960s hippie movement. During the infamous "Summer of Love" in 1967 more than 100,000 people keen to experience "free love" streamed into Haight-Ashbury from all over the US and other parts of the world.

In the neighborhood Haight-Ashbury has long been the most tolerant section of an extremely tolerant city and remains something of a center of alternative lifestyles today. Vintage clothing outlets, alternative bookstores and music stores can still be found on street corners, although today they stand alongside upmarket clothing outlets, chic bars and renowned restaurants.

Clockwise from far left: Fresh fruit and vegetables at the Haight Street Market; Detail of colourful murals in the Haight-Ashbury District

On the streets Strolling around the Haight, it is impossible not to notice the hundreds of elegant Victorian homes that survived the 1906 earthquake, particularly around the intersection of Haight and Ashbury, as well as the colorful murals, predominantly along Haight Street. Wander past the Grateful Dead house at 710 Ashbury Street, where the band lived in the mid-60s, and see the original Hell's Angels HQ at number 719. Janis Joplin lived at 122 Lyon Street and Jefferson Airplane at 2400 Fulton.

Up to the park A walk or jog up to the top of the hill of Buena Vista Park, the oldest park in San Francisco, will reward you with fine views of the city. Ancient oaks and native Monterey Cypress line its many winding trails, and it's also a haven for wildlife.

THE BASICS

🚩 J7

🚌 6, 33, 43, 66, 71

♿ Range from excellent to none depending on location

🆓 Free

www.sfgate.com/neighborhoods/sf/haight

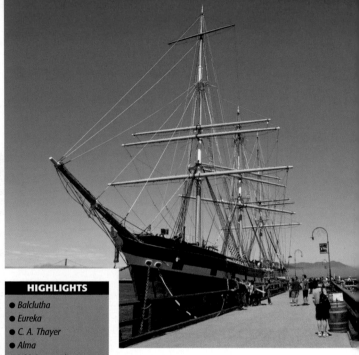

HIGHLIGHTS

- Balclutha
- Eureka
- C. A. Thayer
- Alma
- USS Pampanito
- Eppleton Hall
- Maritime bookstore

TIP

- Currently only the lobby and scenic veranda of the nearby art deco Maritime Museum (Beach Street, at the foot of Polk Street) are open, displaying a few models and paintings of ships, and the newly restored vibrant lobby murals. Renovations of the upper floors will take several years,.

San Francisco was long the hub of the West Coast's maritime trade, and the vessels docked at Hyde Street Pier, as part of the San Francisco Maritime National Historical Park, provide a reminder of the city's seafaring heyday.

Cape Horn veteran The grandest of the ships is the *Balclutha*, a steel-hulled, square-rigged ship launched in Scotland in 1886. This vessel, originally intended to carry wheat between California and Europe, rounded Cape Horn 17 times before ending its days transporting Alaskan salmon along the West Coast. Clamber down the ladders and around the decks for a look at the restored cabins, including the elegant saloon enjoyed by the ship's master, and to read the informative explanatory texts.

Clockwise from far left: The 1895 schooner C. A. Thayer; the square-rigged Balclutha *transported wheat between Europe and California; people walk past a large model of an old sea dog; the* Balclutha, *docked at Hyde Street Pier*

Boats of the bay The 1940s cars and trucks on the lower decks of the *Eureka* suggest the era when the vessel was the world's largest passenger ferry and able to haul 2,300 people and 120 vehicles between San Francisco and Sausalito in a single trip. The other exhibits are the *C. A. Thayer*, built in 1895 to move the lumber used in the construction of many early Californian cities; a 1907 deep-water steam tug, *Hercules*; a paddle tug dating from 1914, *Eppleton Hall*, which spent its working life towing barges in Britain; and the *Alma*, a scow schooner built in 1891, whose flat bottom enabled her to navigate the shallow waters of the bay. The restored USS *Pampanito*, a World War II submarine that made six patrols in the Pacific, is part of the National Park but located at Pier 45.

THE BASICS

www.nps.gov/safr/index.htm

www.maritime.org

✚ N1

✉ Aquatic Park, Hyde Street

☎ 415/447–5000

🕐 Daily 10–5

🚌 19, 30; Hyde–Powell cable car

♿ Few

🎫 Various

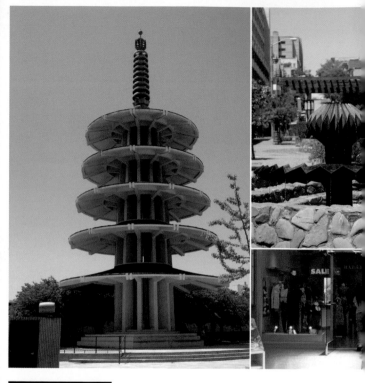

HIGHLIGHTS

- National Japanese American Historical Society
- Japan Center
- Cherry Blossom Festival

TIP

- For two weekends in April, Japantown comes alive with the annual Cherry Blossom Festival, featuring a street fair of Japanese arts and crafts, martial artists, *taiko* drummers and cooking demonstrations.

Today, comparatively few Japanese live in Japantown, bordered by Octavia and Fillmore streets, and O'Farrell and Pine streets, but it's still the spiritual home of San Francisco's Japanese-Americans.

History Established in the late 1800s, San Francisco's Japanese-American community was the first in the US, spanning 30 blocks of the Western Addition. In 1941 almost all the city's 7,000 Japanese-Americans lived and worked here. America's entry into World War II, following the Japanese attack on Pearl Harbor, led to the government's forced internment of the US's Japanese citizens; when the war ended many didn't return to Japantown. California passed legislation in 2001 to preserve the three remaining Japantowns in the state.

Clockwise from far left: The Peace Pagoda stands out against a brilliant-blue sky; the unusual Origami Fountain; taking a break at the Japan Center; if you fancy some Japanese cuisine, there are plenty of restaurants to choose from; a clothes store in the Japan Center

Exhibits and shops At the National Japanese American Historical Society (▷ 72) you can explore the Japanese-American experience. The area's commercial hub is the large Japan Center (Post and Buchanan streets), two indoor malls connected by Peace Plaza. The Miyako and Kintetsu malls house Japanese restaurants and shops selling everything from samurai figurines to Japanese books and foods.

Japanese architecture Across Post Street is the pedestrian-only block of Buchanan Street designed by Japanese-American Ruth Asawa. Several churches have Japanese-style architecture, including Soto Zen Mission Sokoji (Laguna Street), Konko Church of San Francisco (Bush Street), founded in 1931, and the Buddhist Church of San Francisco (1881 Pine Street).

THE BASICS

www.sfjapantown.org
www.njahs.org

🔲 L5

🍴 Plenty of choice, including Mifune (▷ 147)

🚍 2, 3, 22, 38

HIGHLIGHTS

- *Old Man*, de La Tour
- *The Tribute Money*, Rubens
- *St. John the Baptist*, El Greco
- *The Thinker*, Rodin
- *The Three Shades*, Rodin
- *Trotting Horse*, Degas
- *The Grand Canal, Venice*, Monet
- *View of Golden Gate*

Rodin and San Francisco may seem an unlikely combination, but fans of the French sculptor enjoy a visit to this hill-top building that has many of his works amid a fine collection of European art.

Sugar money The collection in the Legion of Honor (modeled on the Légion d'Honneur Museum in Paris) was started in the 1910s by Alma Spreckels, wife of millionaire San Franciscan sugar magnate, Adolph. Already passionate about European art, Alma met Rodin in Paris and so began a lasting interest in his work. Her husband, meanwhile, was motivated to open an art museum through his bitter rivalry with another prominent San Franciscan family, the de Youngs, who had founded the de Young Museum (▷ 28–29).

Clockwise from far left: Rodin's *The Thinker ponders life in the Court of Honor; sculpture on display in Gallery 10; paintings in Gallery 18; artworks in the Early Northern European Gallery; a view of the museum from across the pond*

THE KATHARINE HANRAHAN GALLERY

The collections *The Three Shades* and *The Thinker* stand in the grounds, and some 70 other Rodin works are inside the museum. The general galleries, meanwhile, are arranged in a chronological sequence from the medieval period to the early 20th century, with the highlights mostly from the 18th and 19th centuries. Downstairs, the Achenbach Foundation for Graphic Arts holds more than 100,000 prints and some 3,000 drawings by artists as diverse as Albrecht Dürer and Georgia O'Keeffe, and selections are shown in short-term exhibitions (otherwise by appointment). The Legion also gets first-rate traveling exhibitions; recent ones have included the Magna Carta, on loan from Oxford's Bodleian Library. Outside, beside the parking lot, be sure to see George Segal's *Holocaust* sculpture.

THE BASICS

http://legionofhonor.famsf.org

✚ B5

✉ Lincoln Park

☎ 415/750–3600

🕐 Tue–Sun 9.30–5.15

🍴 Café

🚌 1, 2, 18, 38

♿ Good

💰 Moderate; free 1st Tue of month

❓ Audio and guided tours available

DID YOU KNOW?

● Full name: Misión San Francisco de Asís
● Founded: 1776
● Building commenced: 1782
● Building completed: 1791
● Length: 114ft (35m)
● Width: 22ft (7m)
● Thickness of walls: 4ft (1.5m)
● Number of adobe bricks: 36,000
● First earthquake-proofing measures: 1918

Evidence of the 18th-century Spanish settle-ment of California rarely surfaces in today's San Francisco, but Mission Dolores, the oldest building in the city, provides visitors with a welcome insight into the era.

California's missions The mission was the sixth in a chain of 21 built by the Spanish across California. From San Diego to Sonoma, each mission was located a day's horse ride from the next. The Spaniards' intention was to convert Native Americans to Catholicism, to utilize their labor and to earn their support in colonial conflict. Mexico's independence from Spain in 1821 put the sparsely populated California in Mexican hands, and resulted in the decline and secularization of many of the missions. Most were restored by the US government.

Clockwise from far left: A statue of Junipero Serra stands amid the trees and flowers; the newer basilica, with its ornate Churrigueresque facade, was completed in 1918; sculptures adorn the basilica's exterior; inside the 18th-century chapel

Inside the mission Passing through the thick adobe walls, largely responsible for the mission's success in withstanding numerous earthquakes, you enter the small and richly atmospheric chapel, which has an altar dating from 1780 and is decorated with frescoes by Native Americans. A modest assortment of historic pieces is gathered in the mission's museum, the oldest being a baptismal register for 1776. In the cemetery, headstones mark Spanish- and Mexican-era notables, while the Lourdes Grotto indicates the common grave of some 5,000 Native Americans—many of whom were killed by diseases brought by the colonists. Next to the chapel is the far larger basilica, completed in 1918, now used for Sunday Mass and most weddings; the chapel is used for daily Mass and baptisms.

THE BASICS

www.missiondolores.org

✚ M8

✉ 320 Dolores Street (entrance 3321 16th Street)

☎ 415/621–8203

🕐 Daily 9–4 (May–Oct until 4.30)

🚇 16th Street–Mission

🚌 33, 49

♿ Few

💲 Donation

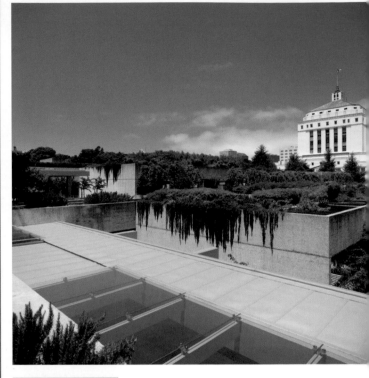

HIGHLIGHTS

- *Yosemite Valley*, Bierstadt
- Diebenkorn paintings
- *Migrant Mother*, Lange
- *San Francisco, July 1849*, Burgess
- Interactive animation and sound-effects studios
- 1913 Cadillac
- 1925 gas pump
- Sculpture garden

TIP

- For advice on sensible precautions to take when in Oakland, ▷ 169–170.

If you cross the San Francisco Bay, don't ignore Oakland. It's home to this superb museum, which leads the way in documenting the history, nature and art of the Golden State.

History Every episode in California's past is remembered here. The collections are enhanced by computers providing recorded commentaries from experts. From outlining the conflicts between Californians and the colonizing Spaniards, the collections come up to date with the rise of Californian computer companies, the invention of the mountain bike and the role of Hollywood.

Californian art An imaginative selection of exhibits demonstrates how the art of California

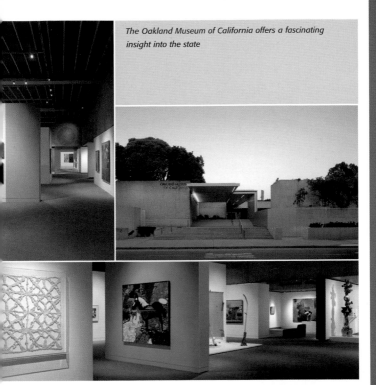

The Oakland Museum of California offers a fascinating insight into the state

has developed from 19th-century depictions of its untamed, natural beauty, through to the self-confidence of 20th-century artists such as semi-abstract painter Richard Diebenkorn and ceramicist Peter Voulkos. The photography collection has outstanding contributions from Dorothea Lange and Maynard Dixon, both of whom were based in San Francisco.

Nature The Gallery of California Natural Sciences has seven sections showcasing the different habitats in California. It's your chance to explore the remarkable plant and animal life found in the high mountains, low deserts, beneath the ocean and in the other habitats of California. Also, take time to explore the peaceful outdoor sculpture garden, with its views of Lake Merritt.

THE BASICS

www.museumca.org
🚹 Off map to east
✉ 1000 Oak Street, Oakland
☎ 510/238–2200, 888/625–6873
🕐 Wed–Thu, Sat–Sun 11–5, Fri 11–9
🍴 Café
🚇 Lake Merritt
♿ Excellent
💲 Moderate; free 1st Sun of month
❓ Free tours. Films, lectures and events

DID YOU KNOW?

* Architect: Bernard Maybeck
* Built: 1915
* Inspirations: Böcklin's *Isle of the Dead*; the drawings of Piranesi
* Materials: originally plaster and wood on a chicken-wire frame
* Height of rotunda: 160ft (49m)
* First restoration: 1964–1975
* Second restoration completed: 2010
* Original cost: $621,929

The Palace of Fine Arts is one of the most beautiful structures in San Francisco. Remarkably, it was intentionally built as a ruin and serves no practical purpose whatsoever.

Architects' playtime In 1915, ostensibly to mark the opening of the Panama Canal, San Francisco announced its recovery from the devastation of the 1906 earthquake and fire by staging the Panama Pacific International Exposition. A group of noted architects was commissioned to erect temporary structures to house the Expo on land reclaimed from the bay. One of the architects was Bernard Maybeck, and it was his Palace of Fine Arts more than any other building that captured the imagination of the Expo's 19 million visitors.

The Palace of Fine Arts was not intended to be a permanent feature of the city when it was built in 1915, but it captured the imagination of San Franciscans and visitors alike

TOP 25

Although it was intended as a temporary structure and was built mostly of plaster and chicken wire, the Palace of Fine Arts aroused such public affection that it was preserved and then, in the 1960s, replicated in concrete at a cost of $7.5 million. In 2010, a $21-million restoration, which included a new dome roof, landscaping and seismic upgrades, was completed.

Art in ruins Maybeck designed a Roman ruin, using a classical domed rotunda as the structure's centerpiece and flanking this with a fragmented colonnade. Each group of columns was topped by weeping maidens and decorated by stairways and huge urns. The intention was to prepare visitors for the classical art exhibited in the Expo's Great Hall, which until recently housed the Exploratorium, ▷ 30–31).

THE BASICS

www.lovethepalace.org

J2

3601 Lyon Street

Always open

28, 30

None

Free

22 San Francisco Museum of Modern Art

HIGHLIGHTS

- *Woman with the Hat*, Matisse
- *Woman*, Willem de Kooning
- *Land's End*, Jasper Johns
- *Guardians of the Secret*, Pollock
- *Violin and Candlestick*, Braque
- Paul Klee drawings
- *The Flower Carrier*, Rivera
- Clyfford Still gallery
- East European photography
- The rooftop garden

Striking and sympathetic architecture, outstanding collections and innovative temporary exhibitions make SFMOMA a showplace befitting a forward-thinking city.

On the move Between summer 2013 and 2016, the museum is undergoing an expansion that will more than double it in size. During this time, a series of traveling and site-specific exhibitions and programs will be held in locations around the bay area. Highlights include exhibitions at the Contemporary Jewish Museum and the Yerba Buena Center for the Arts. Check the museum website for latest information.

Main attraction The core of the museum's permanent collection highlights painting and sculpture from 1900 to 1970. Among

Clockwise from far left: The museum looms up behind a sculpture of an upturned ship, by John Roloff, in Yerba Buena Gardens; giant columns in the atrium; the rooftop garden pavilion; looking up through a futuristic bridge to the sky above

significant contributions from Europeans are Pablo Picasso's *Head in Three-quarter View* and *The Coffee Pot,* and Georges Braque's *Violin and Candlestick.* Do not miss Matisse's *Woman with the Hat*, painted in 1905; a work that made a crucial contribution to what became the century's first radical art movement—fauvism.

Other galleries The canvases of Richard Diebenkorn have particular relevance to the region, as do the 28 works donated by California-based abstract expressionist Clyfford Still. The Phyllis Wattis Theater (main floor) is the place for film screenings, artist lectures and other presentations. The museum is also equipped to stage provocative exhibitions in the emerging fields of video, computer and interactive art.

THE BASICS

www.sfmoma.org

➕ Q5

✉ 151 3rd Street

☎ 415/357–4000

🕐 Sun–Tue, Fri–Sat 10–5.45, Thu 10–8.45; shorter hours in winter

🍴 2 cafés

Ⓜ Montgomery

🚌 12, 30, 45, 76

♿ Excellent

💲 Expensive; free 1st Tue of month

DID YOU KNOW?

● Architect: William L.
Pereira & Associates
● Smallest floor: 48th,
45ft (14m) per side
● Largest floor: 5th,
145ft (44m) per side
● Angle of slope: 5 degrees
● Number of floors: 48

TIP

● Transamerica Redwood
Park, behind the
Transamerica Pyramid,
stages free lunchtime
concerts on weekdays.

A recognized landmark worldwide, the
Transamerica Pyramid is San Francisco's
most distinctive building and arguably the
most innovative modern contribution to
the city's skyline.

Perfect profile With a construction cost of
$32 million, San Franciscans were slow to
appreciate the splendor of the 853ft-high
(260m) building's unique profile. Rising above
the Financial District's forest of even-sided
high-rises, with a slowly tapering spire flanked
by windowless wings and with a decorative
spire rising for 212ft (65m) above the 48th
floor, the Transamerica Pyramid adds greatly
to the city skyline and has steadily been
accepted since 1972. The current owner is the
Dutch insurance company Aegon, who acquired

The Transamerica Pyramid dominates the San Francisco skyline, by day and by night

the Transamerica corporation, which grew from various companies built around the Bank of Italy (later renamed the Bank of America), which was established in San Francisco in 1904.

Inside Construction took place between 1969 and 1972. To help withstand earthquakes, the structure sits on a steel and concrete block sunk 50ft (15m) into the ground. It has 18 elevators, two of which go right to the top, and 3,678 windows. The building is a place of business for more than 1,500 employees of the 50 different firms who rent its space. Since September 11, 2001, unfortunately, the lobby and building have been closed to the general public, so the bird's-eye views of the city are no longer accessible, and visitors must admire the structure from afar.

THE BASICS

www.thepyramidcenter.
com
⊞ Q4
✉ 600 Montgomery
Street
🕐 Open to employees
and their approved guests
only
🚌 30, 41
❓ Lobby and building
closed to visitors post-9/11

HIGHLIGHTS

- Sproul Plaza
- Campanile (also called Sather Tower—carillon recitals on Sunday afternoons)
- Hearst Mining Building
- Phoebe A. Hearst Museum of Anthropology
- Berkeley Art Museum and the Pacific Film Archive
- Sather Gate
- Lawrence Hall of Science
- Morrison Library
- Bancroft Library

A haven of 1960s student dissent, the University of California Berkeley campus might be less radical than it once was, but its buildings and museums and the picture it provides of contemporary student life easily justify a trip.

Past The first college at Berkeley opened in the 1850s, but a lack of funds allowed the facility to be purchased in 1873 by the state government as the first of what are now 10 campuses of the University of California. Much of the university's early finance came as donations from Phoebe Apperson Hearst, wife of a wealthy mining baron and mother of the even more wealthy publishing tycoon William Randolph Hearst. In the 1940s, Robert Oppenheimer was UC Berkeley's professor of physics before moving

Clockwise from far left: The Haas School of Business, at the east side of the campus; the Commencement Convocation at the Greek Theatre marks the pinnacle of the students' achievements; Sather Gate and the Campanile; the Heyns Reading Room, in the Doe Library

to Los Alamos to work on the first atomic bomb. In 1964 the seeds of what evolved into countrywide student rebellions were sown by the sit-ins and rallies of Berkeley's Free Speech Movement.

Present UC Berkeley's 35,000 or so students are now more interested in acquiring a good degree than radical politics, though there is no shortage of campaigns being promoted along Sproul Plaza, in the heart of the campus. Elsewhere on the 178-acre (72ha) campus are museums, libraries and architecturally distinguished buildings, such as John Galen Howard's beaux-arts-style Hearst Mining Building. Howard was also responsible for the elegant Sather Gate, marking the main entrance to the campus opposite Telegraph Avenue.

THE BASICS

www.berkeley.edu
➕ Off map to northeast
✉ Main Gate, Bancroft Way
☎ 510/642-5215
🕐 Daylight hours recommended. Tours Mon–Sat 10, Sun 1
🚊 Berkeley
♿ Good
🎫 Free
❓ The Berkeley Art Museum and Pacific Film Archive (www.bampfa.berkeley.edu) are open for tours and performances. See website for details

HIGHLIGHTS

An infusion of culture in the shadow of Financial District towers, Yerba Buena Gardens are the green heart of a still-evolving tract that mixes museums and arts venues with commercial spaces.

The past In the 1970s, declining manufacturing industries were encouraged to vacate the factories south of Market Street. The opening of the Moscone Convention Center in 1981 became the first step in the regeneration of an under-exploited area within walking distance of the city center.

The present Snaking through the landscaped greenery of Yerba Buena Gardens, the Esplanade is decorated with wacky sculptures and passes an artificial waterfall enclosing a

Yerba Buena Gardens offer the chance to take time out from the bustle of city life. Highlights include the Martin Luther King, Jr. Memorial (below, behind the waterfall), and a range of museums and other cultural venues

monument to Martin Luther King. Adjacent, the Center for the Arts was completed in the mid-1990s with a 775-seat theater, an outdoor auditorium and several galleries with exhibitions of contemporary art. Across Third Street rises the landmark Museum of Modern Art (▷ 56–57). The gray block of the Metreon (▷ 136) forms the Garden's west side, close to which a 1916 carousel marks the approach to the Children's Creativity Museum (▷ 67). St. Patrick's Church, built in 1892 for the once-immense Irish population, is across Mission Street.

Latest additions Joining diverse institutions such as the California Historical Society and the Cartoon Art Museum (▷ 66–67) are the city's Contemporary Jewish Museum (▷ 26–27) and the Museum of the African Diaspora (▷ 72).

THE BASICS
www.ybca.org
www.yerbabuenagardens. com
✚ Q5
✉ Bounded by 3rd, 4th, Mission and Howard streets
☎ 415/978-2787
◉ Ask about individual attractions
◎ Montgomery Street or Powell Street
▤ 10, 12, 30, 38, 45
♿ Excellent
💲 Esplanade free; varies for individual attractions

More to See

This section contains other great places to visit if you have more time. Some are in the heart of the city while others are a short journey away, found under Farther Afield. This chapter also has fantastic excursions that you should set aside a whole day for.

MORE TO SEE

In the Heart of the City

555 CALIFORNIA STREET
www.555cal.com
Formerly known as the Bank of America Center, this is a supreme example of inspired 1960s high-rise office architecture. The 52-story building's dark red exterior, dominating the area by day, seems to become almost transparent at sunset.

➕ Q4 ✉ 555 California Street 🚌 1, 30; California Street cable car

ALAMO SQUARE
Perhaps the most photographed view in San Francisco is of the six Victorian homes, or "painted ladies," on the east side of Alamo Square contrasting with the modern towers in the background.

➕ L6 ✉ Bordered by Hayes, Fulton, Scott and Steiner streets 🚌 5, 21, 22, 24

ASIAN ART MUSEUM
www.asianart.org
Housing the largest collection of its kind in the US, this museum was located in Golden Gate Park for many years. It reopened in the city's former main library in 2003,

the larger space enabling many more of its 17,000 objects to be displayed. The exhibits span 6,000 years and diverse cultures and religions, but the major collections are from China and include the oldest dated example of Chinese Buddhist art (AD338), and important items from the Ming Dynasty (1368–1644) and Xuande Era (1426–35). But the smaller and less obvious items can also delight, such as the silver work, wood carvings and textiles from Bhutan, which give a rare insight into this obscure country.

➕ N6 ✉ 200 Larkin Street, Civic Center ☎ 415/581-3500 🕒 Tue–Sun 10–5 (Thu to 9pm) 🚇 Civic Center 🚌 5, 19, 21, 47, 49 ♿ Excellent 💲 Moderate; free 1st Sun of month

CARTOON ART MUSEUM
www.cartoonart.org
Be they from comics, TV or the movies—or culled from the deepest recesses of history—cartoons are accorded the seriousness of art in the changing exhibitions staged here, which seldom fail to be

The exhibits at the Asian Art Museum span 6,000 years

thought-provoking and entertaining. Displays cover artists from Hanna-Barbera to Charles Schulz. The museum has a classroom for cartoon art and a bookstore with books, gifts and prints.

🔲 Q5 ✉ 655 Mission Street ☎ 415/227–8666 🕐 Tue–Sun 11–5 🚇 Montgomery 🚌 Any Market Street bus, also 10, 30, 45 👿 Moderate

CHESTNUT STREET
www.chestnutshop.com
A mix of shops, eateries and bars have given this Marina District street an effervescent mood and a reputation as a haunt of the young, affluent and unattached.

🔲 K–L3 ✉ Between Divisadero and Fillmore streets (for shops and restaurants) 🚌 30

CHILDREN'S CREATIVITY MUSEUM
www.creativity.org
This arts and technology museum, formerly known as Zeum, encourages kids to use interactive exhibits. There are two floors and six studio spaces where visitors

are encouraged to explore their creative side, whether that involves making a music video, sculpting characters out of clay or learning about digital art. In front of the museum, a restored 1906 carousel by Charles Looff—featuring a menagerie of beautifully hand-carved animals—offers rides for all ages.

🔲 Q6 ✉ 221 4th Street ☎ 415/820–3320 🕐 Wed–Sun 10–4 🚌 14, 30, 45 👿 Moderate

CHINATOWN
www.sanfrancisco.chinatown.com
The compact streets and alleyways of Chinatown's 24 history-laden blocks are home to one of the largest Asian communities outside Asia. Several 100-year-old temples, fortune-cookie factories and numerous exotic stores are crammed into one of the city's most energetic and ethnically distinct neighborhoods. The area also has some of the city's best-value restaurants.

🔲 P4 🚌 1, 30, 45; also California Street cable car

Outdoor dining on busy Chestnut Street

Colorful umbrellas and lanterns decorate a shop in Chinatown

CHINESE CULTURE CENTER

www.c-c-c.org

Situated on the third floor of the Hilton San Francisco—which looms above Portsmouth Square and its legions of elderly Chinese men indulging in games of chance.

✚ Q4 ✉ Hilton San Francisco, 750 Kearny Street ☎ 415/986–1822 ◷ Tue–Sat 10–4 🚌 15, 30, 45 ⛏ Free

CHURCH OF SAINTS PETER AND PAUL

www.stspeterpaulsf.org/church

Long the place of worship for North Beach's Italian community, this imposing Romanesque edifice was founded in 1922. The twin spires rise above Washington Square and are evocatively illuminated at night.

✚ P3 ✉ 666 Filbert Street ☎ 415/421–0809 ◷ Usually 7.30am–8pm 🚌 30, 39, 41, 45 ⛏ Free

COLUMBARIUM

www.californios.us/columbarium

The Columbarium (a final resting place for urns holding the ashes of the deceased) is one of the city's most architecturally noteworthy buildings. Designed by British architect Bernard Cahill and opened in 1898, this elegant, four-story Victorian rotunda decorated with stained glass was starting to decay in 1937 when cremations were outlawed here. It's now restored to its former glory.

✚ H6 ✉ 1 Loraine Court ☎ 415/227–0794 ◷ Mon–Fri 8–5 Sat–Sun 10–3 🚌 33, 38

CONSERVATORY OF FLOWERS

www.conservatoryofflowers.org

The Conservatory of Flowers is arranged by themed galleries: aquatic plants, highland tropics, lowland tropics, potted plants and the special exhibits gallery. More than 50 countries and 1,700 plant species from tropical forests are represented.

✚ G7 ✉ JFK Drive, Golden Gate Park ☎ 415/831–2090 ◷ Tue–Sun 10–4 🚌 5, 21, 33, 44, 71, N–Judah ⛏ Moderate; free 1st Tue of month

DIEGO RIVERA GALLERY

www.sfai.edu/diego-rivera-gallery

An immense mural by the Mexican

The Conservatory of Flowers has plants from more than 50 countries

master Diego Rivera sits at one end of this gallery of the highly respected San Francisco Art Institute, while student works line the other three walls.

🏛 N2 ✉ 800 Chestnut Street ☎ 415/771–7020 (Ext. 4410) 🕐 Daily 9–5 🚌 30, 41; Powell–Hyde cable car

FORT MASON CENTER

www.fortmason.org

From the time of San Francisco's 18th-century Spanish *presidio* (or garrison) to the Korean War of the 1950s, Fort Mason served a military role. From 1972, however, the troop barracks were steadily transformed into a vibrant cultural center. Visual arts can be seen at the Museo ItaloAmericano, focusing on Italian-American topics, and the San Francisco Museum of Modern Art Artists Gallery. Photography, painting and sculpture are also likely to be on show at other spaces around the center. Fort Mason is also home to several theaters, including BATS Improv (▷ 133), the Magic Theatre (▷ 135) and the Young Performers Theatre.

🏛 M2 ✉ Marina Boulevard at Laguna Street (cars enter at Marina Boulevard at Buchanan Street) ☎ 415/345–7500 🕐 Individual museums and galleries vary 🍴 Greens vegetarian restaurant (▷ 145) 🚌 22, 28, 30, 49 ♿ Few 💲 Individual museums free or inexpensive

FORT POINT NATIONAL HISTORIC SITE

www.nps.gov/fopo

Completed in 1861, Fort Point was intended to deter enemy incursions into San Francisco Bay during the Civil War and World War II but never a shot was fired in anger. Period-attired guides describe the fort's past.

🏛 F1 ✉ Beneath south end of Golden Gate Bridge ☎ 415/556–1693 🕐 Fri–Sun 10–5 🚌 28, 29, 76

GHIRARDELLI SQUARE

www.ghirardellisq.com

One of Fisherman's Wharf's successful conversions, the red-brick shell of the chocolate factory that opened here in 1893 now holds a strollable complex of

Fort Point National Historic Site

Ghirardelli Square

shops and restaurants.
N2 ⊠ 900 North Point Street
☎ 415/775–5500 🚇 19, 30; Powell–Hyde
cable car

GLIDE MEMORIAL CHURCH
www.glide.org
The Sunday celebration at Glide
is the main draw (Bill Clinton
famously came to a service), as
is the Reverend Cecil Williams.
Being inclusive is the goal, and the
services focus on community,
music and spirituality—you'll be
encouraged to sing along with the
Glide Ensemble and the eight-
piece Change Band, to dance,
and to hold hands with the person
next to you. Note that Glide fills up
fast on Sundays; arrive 30 minutes
early to make sure you get a seat.
P5 ⊠ 300 Ellis Street ☎ 415/674–
6000 🕐 Sun 9am, 11am 🚇 Powell
🚌 27 ✋ Free

HAAS-LILIENTHAL HOUSE
www.sfheritage.org/haas-lilienthal-house
This elaborate 1886 example of
Queen Anne-style architecture
is also the only San Franciscan

Victorian building to retain its
period-furnished rooms.
Knowledgeable tour guides help
bring to life the history and architectural details of the house and
share anecdotes about previous
owners. Today Haas-Lilienthal
is owned by the non-profit San
Francisco Architectural Heritage.
M4 ⊠ 2007 Franklin Street
☎ 415/441–3000 🕐 Guided tours Wed,
Sat 12–3, Sun 11–4 🚌 3, 19, 47
✋ Moderate

HAYES VALLEY
This once-seedy neighborhood
morphed into an attractive shopping and dining destination after
the 1989 Loma Prieta earthquake
damaged the unsightly freeway
that blighted the neighborhood.
High-end restaurants and burger
joints coexist now, along with chic
boutiques and galleries.
M6 ⊠ Hayes Street between Franklin
and Laguna streets 🚌 21

JAPANESE TEA GARDEN
http://japaneseteagardensf.com
Laid out in traditional Japanese

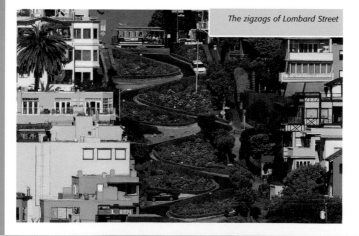
The zigzags of Lombard Street

style, the garden was the work of Makoto Hagiwara, who was interned after the 1941 Japanese attack on Pearl Harbor.

🔲 F7 ✉ Hagiwara Tea Garden Drive and Martin Luther King Jr. Drive ☎ 415/666-3232 🕒 Mar–Oct daily 9–6; Nov–Feb 9–4.45 🚌 5, 21, 33, 44, 71, N–Judah 🖐 Inexpensive

LOMBARD STREET
Traffic zigzags slowly down Lombard Street, "the crookedest street in San Francisco," moving around colorful gardens put in place in the 1920s. On busy summer days, cars back up on Lombard all the way to Van Ness Avenue as drivers wait to head down the crooked street. Go early or late, if possible.

🔲 N2 ✉ Between Hyde and Leavenworth streets 🚌 19, 30

MAIDEN LANE
www.maiden-lane.com
Notorious for its brothels in the 1800s, this road is now lined with smart stores and bordered by fancy white gates. During the late 1940s, architect Frank Lloyd Wright undertook a complete remodeling of 140 Maiden Lane and the design provided a foretaste of his acclaimed Guggenheim Museum in New York. The exterior brickwork is imbued with Mayan motifs; inside is the distinctive spiral ramp.

🔲 Q5 ✉ Between Stockton and Kearny streets 🚌 2, 3, 30, 45

MARINA GREEN
Kite-flying, jogging and dog-walking are popular pursuits in this bayside green strip, overlooked by pastel-colored stucco-fronted houses and serving an affluent neighborhood. This 74-acre (30ha) stretch of grass also offers fantastic views of the Golden Gate Bridge, Alcatraz and Angel Island.

🔲 K–L2 ✉ Beside Marina Boulevard 🚌 22, 76

MISSION DISTRICT MURALS
www.precitaeyes.org, www.balmyalley.com
Some of the best of the Mission District's many murals, reflecting Latin-American muralist traditions, line Balmy Alley and focus on a

Murals on the Women's Building, in the Mission District

theme of peace in Central America. Visit during daylight.

➕ Off map at P9 ✉ Balmy Alley, between 24th and 25th streets ☎ Precita Eyes Mural Center: 415/285-2287 (telephone for tour schedule) 🚌 12, 27, 67

MUSEUM OF THE AFRICAN DIASPORA (MoAD)

www.moadsf.org

Celebrating and exploring the contributions made by those of African descent, MoAD tells its stories through photographs, art, "first voice" narratives, lectures, interactive exhibits and more. Permanent exhibits touch on topics such as slavery, culinary traditions, adornment and music.

➕ Q5 ✉ 685 Mission Street ☎ 415/358-7200 🕐 Wed–Sat 11–6, Sun 12–5 🚌 14, 30, 45 💷 Moderate

NATIONAL JAPANESE AMERICAN HISTORICAL SOCIETY

www.njahs.org

In the heart of Japantown, changing exhibitions here document varied aspects of the Japanese- American life over generations, including the community's contribution to sport, the military, dining and the legacy of unfair internment during World War II.

➕ L5 ✉ 1684 Post Street ☎ 415/921-5007 🕐 Mon–Fri 12–5 and 1st Sat of month 🚌 2, 3, 76

NOB HILL

A quartet of extremely wealthy Californians (the "Big Four") built the first million-dollar mansions on Nob Hill from the 1870s. The 1906 earthquake and fire destroyed all but one of the district's opulent homes, but Nob Hill's pedigree is still evident. The area is home to exclusive hotels and a very well-dressed congregation shows up for Sunday services at the neighborhood's Grace Cathedral (▷ 40–41).

➕ P4 🚌 1, 27; California Street cable car

NORTH BEACH

North Beach's wealth of cafés and bookstores recall its links with the Beat Generation of the 1950s. Meanwhile, the abundant Italian-

Houses on Nob Hill

North Beach has plenty of Italian restaurants

owned restaurants and stores are reminders of the Italians who settled in the district in force from the late 19th century.

➕ P2 🚌 30, 39, 41, 45

OCTAGON HOUSE

www.nscda.org/museums2/ca-octagonhouse

This is one of five eight-sided houses in San Francisco, their shape considered lucky by the owners. The Octagon House dates from 1861 and the restoration program was organized by the Colonial Dames of America, whose exhibitions of Colonial- and Federal-period arts and crafts now fill the interior.

➕ M3 ✉ 2645 Gough Street
☎ 415/441–7512 🕒 Tour 2nd Sun and 2nd and 4th Thu of month 12–3 🚌 41, 45
✋ Free

OLD ST. MARY'S CATHEDRAL

www.oldsaintmarys.org

The West Coast's first Catholic cathedral and the forerunner of today's ultramodern St. Mary's Cathedral (▷ this page), Old

St. Mary's was completed in 1854.

➕ Q4 ✉ 660 California Street ☎ 415/288–3800 🕒 Mon–Fri, Sun 7.30–6, Sat 12–6 🚌 1, 30; California Street cable car
✋ Free

ST. MARY'S CATHEDRAL

www.stmarycathedralsf.org

The cathedral's towering, gleaming-white hyperbolic paraboloids give it a ceiling 194ft (59m) high and form the shape of a Greek cross. Inside, the open-plan cathedral can seat 2,400 people. Its design is intended to eliminate the usual divisions between a cathedral's different areas. Here, the apse, nave, transepts, baptistery and narthex are undivided beneath the tall ceiling, in the center of which is a skylight in the shape of the Cross. The floor to ceiling stained-glass windows in each main wall represent the four elements. To avoid interrupting Mass, call ahead for the schedule.

➕ M5 ✉ 1111 Gough Street
☎ 415/567–2020 🕒 Mon–Sat 6.45–5, Sun 7.30–5 🚌 2, 3, 38 ♿ Excellent
✋ Free

Old St. Mary's Cathedral...

...and the strikingly modern St. Mary's Cathedral

SAN FRANCISCO BOTANICAL GARDEN AT STRYBING ARBORETUM

www.sfbotanicalgarden.org

More than 7,500 varieties of outdoor plants from around the globe fill 55 tended acres (22ha). See the state's famous redwoods on the Redwood Trail.

🚼 F8 ⊠ Ninth Avenue at Lincoln Way ☎ 415/661–1316 🕒 Apr–Oct daily 9–6; Nov–Mar 10–5 🚌 44, 71, N–Judah ✋ Moderate

SUTRO HEIGHTS PARK

From the former grounds of the home of legendary 19th-century San Francisco benefactor Adolph Sutro are fabulous views of the Pacific coast and the western end of Golden Gate Park. Remnants of the house and its statuary are scattered about the park.

🚼 A6 ⊠ Bordered by Point Lobos Avenue, Great Highway and 48th Street 🚌 18, 38

TEMPLE EMANU-EL

www.emanuelsf.org

This immense Byzantine-style structure looms above the surrounding residential architecture. Finished in 1926 at a cost of $3 million, the temple serves the longest-established Jewish congregation in the Bay Area.

🚼 H5 ⊠ Lake Street and Arguello Boulevard ☎ 415/751–2535 🕒 Call for guided tour information 🚌 1, 33 ✋ Free

UNION STREET

The affluent, fashionable residents of Pacific Heights shop, eat and socialize along these chic blocks. The charming Victorian setting makes shopping here a delight.

🚼 L3 ⊠ Between Franklin and Steiner streets 🚌 22, 41, 45

THE WALT DISNEY FAMILY MUSEUM

www.waltdisney.org

Parents might hear "Disney" and assume this museum is for kids, but while there are animated clips and interactive elements that kids will like, the exhibits on the life of Walt Disney will be more interesting to adults. The 10 galleries focus on his life, from his art classes in Kansas City, Missouri, to the creation of Mickey Mouse. Highlights include an elaborate model of Disneyland and lots of audio and video clips. A downstairs screening room shows Disney classics twice daily (extra charge).

🚼 H2 ⊠ 104 Montgomery Street, the Presidio ☎ 415/345–6800 🕒 Wed–Mon 10–6 🚌 43 ✋ Excellent 💲 Expensive

WELLS FARGO MUSEUM

www.wellsfargohistory.com/museums

A leading US financial institution, the name of Wells Fargo is synonymous with the early days of the American West, and this collection demonstrates these historic links. A few steps from the site of the company's 1852 office, the Wells Fargo Museum (inside the Wells Fargo Bank) entertainingly documents the rise of the company. Sitting inside an 1860s stagecoach provides one highlight, but there is much more to see amid the clutter of a re-created Gold Rush-era Wells Fargo office: gold-weighing scales, bulky mining tools, gold coins and aging letters that miraculously survived their trip across the rutted tracks of the old West.

🚼 Q4 ⊠ 420 Montgomery Street ☎ 415/396–2619 🕒 Mon–Fri 9–5 🚌 1, 41; California Street cable car ✋ Good 💲 Free

Farther Afield

ANGEL ISLAND STATE PARK
http://angelisland.org
For a day in the wilds, make the short ferry crossing from Fisherman's Wharf to the mile-square (2.5sq km) Angel Island. The largest piece of land in San Francisco Bay, the island is a state park with paths and bicycle trails. You can also visit a former immigration processing center and see the remains of a military prison. Ferry companies sailing to the island include Tiburon Ferry, Blue & Gold Fleet, and Hornblower Cruises.
➕ Off map to north ✉ 1 mile (1.5km) south of Tiburon Peninsula ☎ 415/435–5390 🕐 Daily 8am–dusk 💷 Expensive (fee for ferries)

CASTRO
www.castrosf.org
The Castro neighborhood, near Noe Valley and the Mission, flies its gay flag proudly—and literally. Castro Street, the main drag, has restaurants, gay bars (including Twin Peaks Tavern, one of the oldest gay bars in the city, at 401 Castro) and the illustrious Castro Theatre (▷ 133). In the 1970s the street was home to Harvey Milk's camera shop, which doubled as his campaign headquarters.
➕ L9 ✉ Castro Street 🚌 24, 33, 35, 37, F, L, K

NOE VALLEY
Strollers (pushchairs) and dogs abound in this neighborhood near the Mission District. The commercial stretch is 24th Street, with tempting restaurants and shops selling everything from high-end cheeses to Latin-American imports.
➕ Off map to south ✉ 24th Street between Guerrero and Diamond streets 🚌 24, 35, 48, J–Church

SAN FRANCISCO ZOO
www.sfzoo.org
Awkwardly located on the fringes of the city, this zoo holds the usual complement of creatures, plus Penguin Island.
➕ Off map to southwest ✉ Sloat Boulevard and 45th Avenue ☎ 415/753–7080 🕐 Mid-Mar to early Nov daily 10–5; early Nov to mid-Mar 10–4 🚌 18, 23, L 💷 Expensive

The former Immigration Station at Angel Island State Park

Penguins are among the animals you can see at San Francisco Zoo

Excursions

SAN JOSE

www.sanjose.org

California's third-largest city, San Jose is also known as the "capital" of Silicon Valley. After a dramatic population and housing boom in the latter half of the 20th century, San Jose's primary industry shifted from agriculture to high-tech. Today San Jose has a larger population than San Francisco and has some sights worth visiting.

San Jose's Tech Museum of Innovation features interactive exhibits organized by themes including innovation, renewable energy, the human body and exploration. The museum also houses an IMAX Dome Theater. The Rosicrucian Egyptian Museum and Planetarium displays an intriguing assemblage of amulets, mummies, textiles, scrolls and other antiquities from the cultures of Assyria, Babylon and Egypt.

Travelers with kids could stop by the Winchester Mystery House. Widow and rifle heiress Sarah Winchester believed that the spirits of those killed by Winchester weapons haunted her; if her house was ever completed, she was certain she would die. So her carpenters spent 38 years building this 160-room Victorian mansion. There are stairways to nowhere and windows that open to blank walls, plus 47 fireplaces.

Nearby is Santana Row (between Olsen Drive and Stevens Creek Boulevard), a shopping and entertainment destination with nearly two dozen restaurants, 70 stores and a luxurious day spa.

Winchester Mystery House

Distance: 50 miles (80km) south of San Francisco
Journey Time: 1 hour
Route: Take US 280 south to the Vine Street/Almaden Boulevard exit. Turn left onto Almaden Boulevard
🚇 408 Almaden Boulevard ☎ 408/295–9600 or 800/726–5673
Tech Museum of Innovation
www.thetech.org
✉ 201 South Market Street ☎ 408/294–8324 🕐 Daily 10–5 ✋ Moderate
Rosicrucian Egyptian Museum and Planetarium
www.egyptianmuseum.org
✉ 1660 Park Avenue ☎ 408/947–3635
🕐 Wed–Thu 9–5, Fri 9–8, Sat–Sun 10–6 ✋ Moderate
Winchester Mystery House
www.winchestermysteryhouse.com
✉ 525 South Winchester Boulevard
☎ 408/247–2101 🕐 Daily at 8am (summer), 9am (winter); closing time varies ✋ Expensive

SAUSALITO

www.sausalito.org

Once inundated with fishermen, bordellos and gambling dens, Sausalito has morphed into a summer escape for the elite of San Francisco, which these days thrives on tourism.

Bridgeway is the main thorough-fare, running along the promenade past the ferry landing and shops, which include a number of galleries. The street also has waterfront restaurants. The Bay Model Visitor Center, on Marinship Way, is a replica of the San Francisco Bay and a scientific tool operated by the US Army Corps of Engineers. The Bay Area Discovery Museum on McReynolds Road has interactive exhibits and multimedia labs to entice children to learn about art, science and media. Its Lookout Cove also has 2.5 acres (1ha) of space for outdoor playing.

Over at Cavallo Point resort, adults can improve their culinary skills at the Cavallo Point Cooking School or enjoy the lauded Murray Circle restaurant. Visitors can also hike around Fort Baker, under the Golden Gate Bridge.

Frigid temperatures in the San Francisco Bay make swimming an activity to avoid, but Sea Trek Sausalito rents single and double kayaks and offers guided trips.

Distance: 12 miles (19km) north of San Francisco
Journey Time: 30 minutes
Route: Take US 101 north, exit at Alexander Avenue on the north end of the Golden Gate Bridge. Follow signs to downtown Sausalito ℹ️ 780 Bridgeway ☎ 415/332–0505 🚢 Blue & Gold Fleet from Pier 39 at Fisherman's Wharf or the Golden Gate Ferry

departing from the San Francisco Ferry Building 🚌 Golden Gate Transit Bus 10

Bay Model Visitor Center

www.spn.usace.army.mil

✉ Marinship Way, parallel to Bridgeway ☎ 415/332–3871 🕐 Jun–Aug Tue–Fri 9–4, Sat–Sun 10–5; Sep–May Tue–Sat 9–4 💰 Free

Bay Area Discovery Museum

www.baykidsmuseum.org

✉ 557 McReynolds Road ☎ 415/339–3900 🕐 Tue–Fri 9–4, Sat–Sun 10–5 💰 Moderate

Cavallo Point

www.cavallopoint.com

✉ 601 Murray Circle
☎ 415/339–4700

Sea Trek Sausalito

www.seatrek.com

✉ Schoonmaker Point Marina (at the end of the marina) ☎ 415/332–8494

An aerial view of Sausalito harbor

SONOMA VALLEY

www.sonomavalley.com

Entire guidebooks are devoted to the Wine Country, but visitors can get a good feel for the region by exploring the lovely Sonoma Valley, which is less commercial than nearby Napa Valley. When visiting vineyards in the area, note that in addition to wine tasting, wineries often have other activities and events, including cave tours, tram rides and food-and-wine pairing dinners. During Wine Country's "crush" harvest season, usually mid-August to October, the area is particularly beautiful, busy and packed with special events. While in the town of Sonoma, explore the Sonoma Mission and the other restored historic buildings, artisan shops and boutiques around Sonoma Plaza. A few minutes from the plaza is Buena Vista Winery and Tasting Room. North of Sonoma is the hamlet of Glen Ellen, where visitors can tour Jack London State Historic Park, the former home of the writer whose name it bears. Continue north to Kenwood, where there are more wineries, including Chateau St. Jean and Kunde Family Estate. About 25 miles (40km) north of Kenwood is the small town of Healdsburg, which has a charming town square, a variety of restaurants and a number of wineries within a 20-minute radius.

For a non-winery detour northwest of Kenwood, head to the town of Santa Rosa, just off Highway 101. There you'll find the Charles M. Schulz Museum and Research Center, which features the art of the cartoonist behind the "Peanuts" strip, and a re-creation of his studio.

Sonoma City Hall

Distance: 45 miles (72km) north of San Francisco
Journey Time: 1 hour
Route: Take the Golden Gate Bridge and continue north on US 101 through San Rafael and follow signs to Sonoma
🛈 453 1st Street East ☎ 866/996–1090 or 707/996–1090

Jack London State Historic Park

www.jacklondonpark.com
✉ 2400 London Ranch Road ☎ 707/938–5216 🕐 Thu–Mon 10–5 💲 Moderate (vehicle fee)

Charles M. Schulz Museum

www.schulzmuseum.org
✉ 2301 Hardies Lane, Santa Rosa
☎ 707/579–4452 💲 Jun–Aug Mon–Fri 11–5, Sat–Sun 10–5; Sep–May Mon, Wed–Fri 11–5, Sat–Sun 10–5

STANFORD UNIVERSITY

www.stanford.edu

Venture south from San Francisco to reach Stanford University, an 8,180-acre (3,310ha) campus in the Silicon Valley featuring sandstone and tile architecture.

While students and locals refer to the school as "the Farm," the prestigious private university has blue blood. Founded by Leland Stanford, a railroad magnate and US senator, in memory of his only son, the university boasts the third-largest endowment in the nation. Famous former students include Chelsea Clinton, Tiger Woods and the founders of HP and Google.

Campus walking tours (lasting 70 minutes) are offered at 11am and 3.15pm daily, except during the university's winter break and other holidays. Tour highlights include the Main Quad, dominated by Hoover Tower. Rising 285ft (87m) and completed in 1941, the tower is named for the country's 31st president, who was a member of the first graduating class of 1895. It was built to mark the university's 50th anniversary. Art-lovers should stop by the Cantor Arts Center and the adjoining Rodin Sculpture Garden. The galleries showcase art spanning the centuries, from the *Torso of Dionysos* (AD50) to Rodin sculptures to modern and contemporary works; an additional 20 bronze Rodin sculptures are on display in the Rodin Sculpture Garden (open 24 hours).

Get lunch on campus at Cool Café, overlooking the Rodin Sculpture Garden.

Distance: 33 miles (53km) south of San Francisco
Journey Time: 40 minutes
Route: Take US 101 south to Embarcadero Road exit heading west toward Stanford. At El Camino Real, turn into Galvez Street as it enters the university. Stay in the left lane and continue to the heart of campus
🛈 Memorial Hall, Serra Street (across from Hoover Tower) ☎ 650/723–2560
Cantor Arts Center
✉ Lomita Drive and Museum Way
☎ 650/723–4177 🕐 Wed, Fri–Sun 11–5, Thu 11–8 🍴 Cool Café 💲 Free

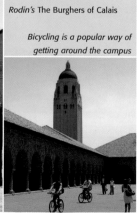

Rodin's The Burghers of Calais

Bicycling is a popular way of getting around the campus

City Tours

This section contains self-guided tours that will help you explore the sights in each of the city's regions. Each tour is designed to take one or two days, with a map pinpointing the recommended places along the way. There is a quick reference guide at the end of each tour, listing everything you need in that region, so you know exactly what's close by.

CITY TOURS

The Presidio

Old meets new in the Presidio, where several remarkable symbols—the Legion of Honor, the Palace of Fine Arts and the famed Golden Gate Bridge—share space with George Lucas's Letterman Digital Arts Center and The Walt Disney Family Museum, the district's most recent addition.

Morning
Begin your tour of the Presidio area with its most iconic landmark, the **Golden Gate Bridge** (▷ 34–35). Head to the base of the span by foot, bike or car, then stroll across the pedestrian lane and take in the city views. Back at the base of the southern edge of the bridge, stop at **Fort Point National Historic Site** (▷ 69) to learn a bit about San Francisco's military history—and to see lovely beach views and an unexpected angle of the bridge: its underbelly.

Mid-Morning
Recharge your batteries at the **Warming Hut** (Presidio Building 983; daily 9–5; longer in summer), a café and bookstore at the western end of Crissy Field, near the Golden Gate Bridge, where you can get a caffeine fix, a snack and buy some souvenirs. It has a warm, homey atmosphere and views of the bridge are great from here. Then head to the picturesque **Palace of Fine Arts** (▷ 54–55) to see the dome, Greek-style colonnades, the duck-filled lagoon and, on weekends, most likely a bridal party taking wedding pictures. On any day of the week, it's the most photographed part of the city.

Lunch
Geary Boulevard is the main artery of the Richmond District, home to ethnic restaurants serving authentic cuisine at reasonable prices. Try **Ton Kiang** (▷ 149) for high-quality dim sum, or stumble on another gem in the area. Clement Street, which runs parallel to Geary, also has good restaurant choices. **Burma Superstar** (309 Clement Street; daily lunch and dinner) always has a wait, for good reason.

CITY TOURS

Afternoon

Investigate more of the **Golden Gate National Recreation Area** (▷ 36–37), a protected area that attracts 17 million visitors annually.

Mid-Afternoon

Wind your way through the Presidio to **The Walt Disney Family Museum** (▷ 74), which chronicles the history and triumphs of one of America's most famous animators. Audio and video footage of Disney, his family, his colleagues and his beloved creations bring him to life. Highlights include drawings, movie clips, a tribute to Snow White and an elaborate model of Disneyland.

Dinner

The best option for dinner is sophisticated **Spruce** (▷ 148–149), in Laurel Heights. While the area isn't known for its nightlife, diners can stay at Spruce for a cocktail in the lively bar area, or check out the **Presidio Social Club** (▷ 148). Families looking for an evening activity could reserve one of the 12 lanes at **Presidio Bowl** (Presidio Building 93, Moraga Avenue and Montgomery Street; Sun–Thu 9am–midnight, Fri–Sat 9am–2am), which also serves food and drinks.

Golden Gate
Bridge

Fort Point
National Historic
Site

Fort Point
Wharf

Warming Hut

Toll Plaza

Hoffman Street

PRESIDIO

Fort
Winfield
Scott

Dynamite Road

Golden Gate National Recreation Area

World War II
Memorial

Presidio

Compton Road

Washington

Baker
Beach

Legion of
Honor

Sea Cliff Avenue

Scenic Way

SEA CLIFF

Mountain
Lake

Mountain
Lake Park

West Clay Street

LAKE STREET

CALIFORNIA

Sutro Anex
Park

Clement Street

Clement

Sutro Heights
Park

Ton Kiang

GEARY BOULEVARD

GEARY

GEARY

CENTRAL RICHMOND

Anza

| 0 | 500 m |
| 0 | 500 yds |

Balboa

San Francisco Bay

Golden Gate National Recreation Area

Crissy Field

Golden Gate Beach

Lagoon

Marine Drive
Jauss Street
Mason Street
MARINA BOULEVARD
Jefferson Street
Yacht Road
Yacht Harbor

Old Mason Street
Mason Street

DOYLE DRIVE

PARKWAY

LINCOLN BOULEVARD
Patten Road

The Walt Disney Family Museum

Young Street
Hallock Street
Evans Avenue
Corgas
101
Palace of Fine Arts
Bay Street
RICHARDSON AVENUE
Baker Street
Broderick Street

National Cemetery

Fisher Loop
Presidio Theater

THE PRESIDIO

Herbst International Exhibition Hall

Presidio Bowl

LINCOLN BOULEVARD
Jerden Avenue
McDowell Avenue
Montgomery Street
Anza Avenue
Graham Street
Keyes Avenue
Mesa Street
Morales
Hardie Place
Barnard Avenue
Thomas Avenue
Infantry Terrace
Crook Street
Presidio Boulevard
Funston Avenue
Presidio Boulevard
MacArthur Avenue
Liggett Avenue
Letterman Drive
Torney Avenue
Lincoln Boulevard
Gorgas Avenue
Sumner

LOMBARD STREET
Sherman Road
Simonds Loop
PRESIDIO BOULEVARD
Simonds Loop
Shafter Road
Lincoln Boulevard
Liggett Avenue
Storey Avenue
Merton Street
Rodriguez Street
Portola Street
El Polin Loop

Presidio Social Club

Greenwich Street
Baker Street
Lyon Street
Broderick Street
Union Street
Green Street
Vallejo Street

National Park

Pinal Loop
Washington Boulevard
Arguello Boulevard

Inspiration Point

Presidio Golf Course

WEST PACIFIC AVENUE
West Pacific Avenue

Arguello Boulevard

Pacific Avenue

PRESIDIO AVENUE
Jackson Street
Baker Street

Swedenborgian Church

Jackson Street
West Pacific Avenue
Maple Street
Spruce Street
Locust Street
Laurel Street
Walnut Street
Clay Street
Sacramento Street

LAKE STREET

Temple Emanu-El

Cherry Street
Arguello Boulevard
2nd Avenue

Washington Street
Clay Street
Sacramento Street

PRESIDIO HEIGHTS

Spruce Street
Spruce Street

CALIFORNIA STREET

San Francisco Fire Department Museum

7th Avenue
5th Avenue
3rd Avenue
STREET
Cornwall Street
4th Avenue
Palm Avenue
ARGUELLO BOULEVARD
Jordan Avenue
Commonwealth Avenue
Parker Avenue
Spruce Street
Mayfair Drive
Iris Avenue
Manzanita Avenue
Heather Avenue
Collins Street
Euclid Avenue
Lupine Avenue
Wood Street
Emerson Street
MASONIC AVENUE
Presidio Avenue
Lyon Street
Baker Street

LAUREL HEIGHTS

Municipal Offices

Burma Superstar

GEARY BOULEVARD

Columbarium

BOULEVARD

INNER RICHMOND

5th Avenue
3rd Avenue
2nd Avenue
Edward Street
Turk Street
ARGUELLO BOULEVARD
Rossi Avenue
Beaumont Avenue
Amsden Court
Parker Avenue
Stanyan Street

Anza Street
Cook Street
Blake Street
Ewing Terrace

University of San Francisco (Lone Mountain Campus)

LONE MOUNTAIN

Turk Street
Turk Terrace
Chabot Terrace
Aspen Terrace
Anza Vista Avenue
Terra Vista Avenue
O'Farrell Street
Vega Street
Encanto Avenue
Nido Avenue
Beideman Avenue
Anza Vista Avenue
Fortuna Avenue
Central Avenue

G   H   J   K

CITY TOURS

85

The Presidio Quick Reference Guide

Golden Gate Bridge (▷ 36)
A magnificent feat of both engineering and beauty, the span connecting San Francisco to Marin County is the most recognizable bridge in the country, if not the world. More than 42 million vehicles cross it every year.

Golden Gate National Recreation Area (▷ 38)
From stunning cliffs to rugged coastline, the GGNRA comprises 75,500 acres (30,553ha) of protected recreational land spanning both sides of the Golden Gate Bridge.

Legion of Honor (▷ 48)
Part of the Fine Arts Museums of San Francisco, this stately hill-top museum houses a fine collection of European art, including more than 70 works by the French sculptor Rodin, along with a diverse collection of prints and drawings.

Palace of Fine Arts (▷ 54)
A much-photographed Roman-style ruin that was built for the Panama Pacific International Exposition in 1915, the Palace of Fine Arts was meant to be a temporary structure , but an adoring city has helped it to survive.

CITY TOURS

The Byzantine-style Temple Emanu-El

CITY TOURS

Pacific Heights to Telegraph Hill

An infamous prison, a soaring monument and a former army barracks rise up in the northern section of the city. Also here are the roots of the Beat Generation and their antithesis: high-end shopping and sprawling homes in Pacific Heights.

Morning
Hop on an early ferry to **Alcatraz** (▷ 14–15), formerly an island prison and now one of San Francisco's most popular tourist destinations (reserve ahead, especially in summer). After a scenic ferry ride, you can tour the prison at your own pace accompanied by an audio tour, with commentary from former guards and inmates.

Mid-Morning
After you return from Alcatraz, explore **Pier 39** (▷ 126) and **Ghirardelli Square** (▷ 69–70), a chocolate factory that was converted into a complex of shops and restaurants in Fisherman's Wharf. Nearby, San Francisco's maritime history is well-documented at **Hyde Street Pier** (▷ 44–45), with its grand historical ships, some of which date as far back as the late 1800s.

Lunch
From Fisherman's Wharf it's a short drive or bus ride to **Chestnut Street** (▷ 67), which has a number of casual options for lunch. Consider flavorful tacos and ceviche at **Tacolicious** (▷ 149) or all-American burgers and fries at **Barney's Gourmet Hamburgers** (▷ 142), which has an enticing patio at the back.

Afternoon
Walk off lunch by window-shopping on Chestnut Street or by strolling along the **Marina Green** (▷ 71), where you can take in views of Alcatraz, Angel Island and the Golden Gate Bridge—and even fly a kite.

Mid-Afternoon
Then head back to Chestnut Street and take the 30 bus toward downtown; the bus will take you straight to the Italian neighborhood of **North Beach** (▷ 72–73). Walk through Washington Square Park en route to steep **Telegraph Hill** (▷ 24–25). Tackle the hill on foot or take bus 39 to reach **Coit Tower** (▷ 24–25), perched at the summit. The fluted concrete column has an observation gallery, but the views from Pioneer Park, at the base of the tower, are also incredible. After you return to North Beach, don't miss **City Lights** (▷ 123), a bookstore that was pivotal to the 1950s Beat Generation.

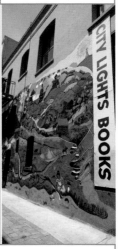

Dinner
There are a number of dinner options, whether you want Italian fare in North Beach or French, Asian or other cuisines on Union or Chestnut streets. New-American fare at **Gary Danko** (▷ 144), on the edge of Fisherman's Wharf, is expensive but worth it.

Evening
The after-dark choices here are plentiful, including live music, comedy, movie theaters and crowded bars (often skewing on the younger side). Consider getting tickets for Beach Blanket Babylon, a show that has run for decades at **Club Fugazi** (▷ 134). For laughs, there's always great improvisation at **BATS Improv** (▷ 133) in Fort Mason.

San Francisco
Maritime National
Historical Park

Municipal
Pier

Alma

Hercules

Balclutha

Eureka

Hyde Street Pier
Historical Ships

CA Thayer

Pier 3

Pier 2

Aquatic
Park

Aquatic Park
Beach

Festival
Pavilion

Pier I

Herbst
Pavilion

San Francisco
National Maritime
Museum

Victoria
Park

FORT
MASON

BATS Improv

Green Drive

Marina

Marina Green

Casa Way

Jefferson
Street

Beach
Street

Gary
Danko

Fort Mason
Center

Rico Way

Museo Italo Americano &
African-American
Cultural Society

Ghirardelli
Square

Mallorca
Way

Alhambra Street

Toledo Way

Great
Meadow

Van
Ness

Polk

Larkin

Russian
Hill Park

BAY

STREET

BAY

North

Point

Street

Laguna

Street

Beach

Street

Pierce
Street

Bay

Street

MARINA

Francisco

Street

George Moscone
Recreation
Center

Chestnut

Street

RUSSIAN HILL

Chestnut
Street

Tacolicious

Magnolia

Street

LOMBARD

STREET

Barney's
Gourmet
Hamburgers

Moulton

Street

101

Street

Greenwich

Street

Pixley

Street

Fillmore

Filbert

Octagon
House

Street

Street

Union
Street

Union

Street

Allyne
Park

Street

VAN

101

COW HOLLOW

Buchanan

Laguna

Green

Gough

Street

Steiner

Webster

Octavia

Franklin

Pierce

Vallejo

NESS

AVENUE

Broadway

Street

BROADWAY

Pacific

Avenue

Street

Jackson

Street

STREET

AVENUE

Haas-Lilienthal
House

Polk

PACIFIC HEIGHTS

Washington

Alta Plaza
Park

Lafayette
Park

Clay

Street

Street

Clay
Theater

Sacramento

Perine
Place

CALIFORNIA

STREET

CALIFORNIA

STREET

Pine

CALIFORNIA

Octavia

Pine

Street

Scott

Pierce

Wilmot

Fillmore

WEBSTER

Street

Bush

Gough

FRANKLIN

Street

VAN

NESS

Sutter

JAPANTOWN

Peace
Pagoda

Post

National Japanese
American Historical
Society

GEARY

BOULEVARD

St Mary's
Cathedral

GEARY

AVENUE

O'Farrell

Cleary
Court

Laguna Street

Ellis

O'Farrell

Street

Hollis
Street

Willow
Street

L

M

Alcatraz,
Angel Island State Park

Pier 45
SS Jeremiah O'Brien
Ferry Dock
USS Pampanito
Pier 41
Pier 43
Pier 39 Complex
Fisherman's Wharf
Pier 43.5
Pier 35
Cruise Ship Terminal
Pier 47
Pier 33
The Embarcadero
The Cannery
Ripley's Museum
Pier 31
Jefferson street
Madame Tussauds and The San Francisco Dungeon
Beach Street
Powell Street
Pier 29
NORTH POINT STREET
Mason Street
Pier 27
BAY STREET
Kearny Street
Historic Streetcar
STREET
Francisco Street
Grant Avenue
Stockton Street
THE EMBARCADERO
Chestnut Street
Chestnut Street
Chestnut Street
COLUMBUS AVENUE
Lombard Street
Lombard Street
Diego Rivera Gallery
Lombard Street
Pioneer Park
Coit Tower
Levi's Plaza
NORTH BEACH
Greenwich Street
Church of Saints Peter and Paul
Washington Square
Filbert Street
TELEGRAPH HILL
Battery Street
Filbert Street
Union Street
NORTHEAST WATERFRONT HISTORIC DISTRICT
Front Street
Union Street
Club Fugazi
Green Street
Green Street
Ina Coolbrith Park
Vallejo Street
COLUMBUS AVENUE
Vallejo Street
BROADWAY STREET
STREET
City Lights
Pacific Avenue
Pacific Avenue
Jackson Street
Cable Car Museum
CHINATOWN
Chinese Culture Center
Transamerica Redwood Park
Chinese Historical Society of America
Pacific Heritage Museum
Transamerica Pyramid
NOB HILL
Clay Street
Old St. Mary's Cathedral
Wells Fargo Museum
FINANCIAL DISTRICT
Fairmont Hotel
Sacramento Street
Huntington Park
CALIFORNIA STREET
California Street
Sansome Street
Grace Cathedral
CALIFORNIA
Pine Street
Powell Street
Bush Street
Stockton Street
Sutter Street
MARKET STREET
Post Street
Maiden Lane
Montgomery Street
0   500 m
0   500 yds
Union Square
Maiden Lane
STREET
GEARY
Cartoon Art Museum
STREET
Museum of the African Diaspora (MoAD)
Glide Memorial Church
O'Farrell Street
Contemporary Jewish Museum
Macaulay Park
Ellis Street
Eddy Street
Westfield San Francisco Center
Yerba Buena Gardens
TENDERLOIN
Powell Street
MARKET STREET
MISSION STREET
Moscone Convention Center
N
P
P
Q

CITY TOURS

91

Pacific Heights to Telegraph Hill
Quick Reference Guide

 SIGHTS AND EXPERIENCES

CITY TOURS

Alcatraz (▷ 14)

For nearly 30 years, "The Rock" was a top-security penitentiary and the country's most feared place of incarceration. Today the former island prison is a popular tourist draw with a colorful history, and the subject of many movies. Visitors can see former cells, the hospital, exercise yard and mess hall, as well as a museum explaining the wider history of the infamous island.

Coit Tower and Telegraph Hill (▷ 24)

A monument perched atop one of San Francisco's famous hills, the 180ft-high (55m) Coit Tower is visible from many parts of the city. Don't miss the 19 frescoed murals inside, or the views from the observation gallery, accessible by elevator. The tower, completed in 1933, was built thanks to a bequest from San Francisco socialite Lillie Hitchcock Coit.

Hyde Street Pier Historical Ships (▷ 44)

Though the city's seafaring heyday is in the past, the vessels docked at Hyde Street Pier serve as an engaging reminder of San Francisco's maritime roots. The most impressive ship is the *Balclutha*, dating from 1886, which rounded Cape Horn no less than 17 times. A World War II submarine is nearby at Pier 45.

CITY TOURS

Downtown to Nob Hill

Downtown is the city's hub for business and shopping, alongside the South of Market (SoMa) district, a first-rate destination for art and culture. Chinatown offers quirky shops and inexpensive food, while Nob Hill retains an elegance of the railroad tycoons who once lived here.

Morning

Start your day with a peek inside **Grace Cathedral** (▷ 40–41), noted for its stained glass, its playful labyrinths and its echoes of France's Notre-Dame. Outside the cathedral, stroll around **Nob Hill** (▷ 72) and relax in Huntington Park before making your way to the **Cable Car Museum** (▷ 16–17), where you can learn more about the charming (and slow!) mode of transportation that's unique to San Francisco.

Mid-Morning

Head down Washington Street toward **Chinatown** (▷ 67), exploring the quirky trinket shops on Grant Avenue. Then return to Washington, continuing east until you spot the **Transamerica Pyramid** (▷ 58–59), a distinctive part of the San Francisco skyline. Unfortunately, the building is no longer open to the general public, so your stop here will be quick. Then stroll around downtown, including a walk down pedestrian-only **Maiden Lane** (▷ 71) to check out the high-end boutiques and galleries; don't miss **Xanadu Gallery** (▷ 127), a Frank Lloyd Wright-designed building.

Lunch

For a casual, reasonably priced lunch, stop by the food court downstairs at the **Westfield San Francisco** center (▷ 127)—the quality is much better and varied than your average mall food court. After lunch, indulge in more shopping in the mall, which is anchored by Bloomingdales and Nordstrom department stores.

Afternoon

The San Franciscco Museum of Modern Art (▷ 56–57) is closed for expansion until 2016 but is hosting satellite exhibitions and events around the Bay Area until then. Take a stroll past its striking building, which houses its ever-expanding collection of 20th-century painting and sculpture. The **Museumstore** and SFMOMA's cafes—one of which is part of the rooftop garden—are worth a visit when open. Wander through the attractive Yerba Buena Gardens (▷ 62–63); its plants, grass and waterfall form-

ing a welcome oasis in the centre of the city. Then take your pick from one of a number of other museums in this area – too many to tackle on one afternoon – according to your interests. There's the **Cartoon Art Museum** (▷ 66–67), the **Museum of the African Diaspora** (MoAD; ▷ 72), the **Contemporary Jewish Museum** (▷ 26–27) or the galleries at **Yerba Buena Gardens** (▷ 62–63).

Early evening

After an afternoon of indoor culture, make a beeline for the **Embarcadero** (▷ 32–33). A walk along the waterfront offers views of the Bay Bridge and outdoor sculpture. The **Ferry Building** (▷ 32–33), with its clock tower and vaulted ceiling, is architecturally interesting.

Dinner

These neighborhoods offer a range of cuisines and prices, from inexpensive Pakistani fare to high-end French food to authentic Chinese. Or you could sample American comfort food at **Wayfare Tavern** (▷ 149). After dinner, have a first-rate cocktail at **Bourbon & Branch** (▷ 133), a former speakeasy; you need to make a reservation online to get the password to enter. Or find out what's on at the respected **American Conservatory Theater** (▷ 132).

CITY TOURS

Lombard Street
Greenwich
Filbert Street
Church of Saints Peter and Paul
NORTH BEACH
Coit Tower
TELEGRAPH HILL

Washington Square
Union Street

Ina Coolbrith Park

BROADWAY

CHINATOWN
Transamerica Pyramid
Chinese Culture Center
Cable Car Museum
Chinese Historical Society of America
Pacific Heritage Museum
Wayfare Tavern
NOB HILL
Old St Mary's Cathedral
Wells Fargo Museum
Fairmont Hotel
Huntington Park
Grace Cathedral
555 California Street

Pine Street
Bush Street
Sutter Street
Post Street

Maiden Lane
Xanadu Gallery
Union Square

GEARY STREET
American Conservatory Theater
Bourbon & Branch
Museum of the African Diaspora (MoAD)
Glide Memorial Church
Contemporary Jewish Museum
Yerba Buena Gardens
Powell Street
Westfield San Francisco Center
Moscone Center (West)
Children's Creativity Museum

TENDERLOIN

Federal Building
State Building
Asian Art Museum
Federal Building
City Hall
Library
Civic Center
Federal Building
SOUTH OF MARKET
South of Market Park
Bill Graham Civic Auditorium

Hall of Justice

96

Pier 17

Pier 15

Pier 9

Exploratorium

**NORTHEAST
WATERFRONT
HISTORIC DISTRICT**

Pier 7

Battery

Front

THE EMBARCADERO

Davis

Pier 3

Pier 1

STREET

St

St

St

Walton
Park

Jackson

Street

WASHINGTON STREET

DRUMM STREET

*Transamerica
Redwood
Park*

Clay Street

Davis

Embarcadero Center

**FINANCIAL
DISTRICT**

STREET

Battery

St

Sansome
Street

STEUART STREET

**Ferry Building &
the Embarcadero**

Embarcadero

**Rincon
Center**

MARKET STREET

Spear Street

Main Street

THE EMBARCADERO

**Oakland Museum of California,
UC Berkeley Campus** →

**Rincon
Towers**

*Rincon
Park*

FREMONT STREET

Beale Street

Stevenson Street

1ST STREET

**TRANSBAY
TEMPORARY
TERMINAL**

Pier 24

Folsom

SAN FRANCISCO - OAKLAND BAY BRIDGE 80

Pier 26

Montgomery
Street

2ND STREET

Tehama Street

Street

Pier 28

**Cartoon Art
Museum**

**San Francisco
Museum of
Modern Art**

3rd Street

Hawthorne Street

STREET

UPPER LEVEL

Pier 30

**SOUTH
BEACH**

Beale Street

THE EMBARCADERO

P

**Bayside
Village**

Pier 32

Pier 34

**Moscone
Convention
Center**

Folsom Street

Delancey Street

Pier 36

JAMES LICK FREEWAY

STREET

Brannan

Pier 38

HARRISON STREET

2ND STREET

*South
Park*

Colin P. Kelly Jr. Street

Pier 40

BRYANT STREET

3rd Street

Ritch Street

STREET

*South Beach
Harbor Park*

**South Beach
Harbor**

4TH STREET

BRANNAN STREET

Street

2nd / King

Freelon Street

STREET

**AT&T Park
Baseball Stadium**

5TH STREET

KING STREET

3rd Street

Street

Townsend

China Basin

**SAN FRANCISCO
CALTRAIN STATION** (R)

P

Berry Street

Street

*China Basin
Park* (S)

0   500 m

0   500 yds

CITY TOURS

97

Downtown to Nob Hill
Quick Reference Guide

CITY TOURS

Cable Car Museum (▷ 16)
Celebrating the city's relatively inefficient—but beloved—form of public transportation, this museum has intriguing memorabilia.

Chinese Historical Society of America (▷ 20)
Learn more about the story of the Chinese in California, including the early Gold Rush days.

Contemporary Jewish Museum (▷ 26)
Located in SoMa, the CJM focuses on contemporary Jewish art, film, music and more.

Ferry Building and the Embarcadero (▷ 32)
Shops and restaurants now fill the historic Ferry Building, on the palm tree-lined Embarcadero.

Grace Cathedral (▷ 40)
This stunning neo-Gothic cathedral was built on the former site of a railroad baron's mansion, in Nob Hill.

San Francisco Museum of Modern Art (▷ 56)
Paintings and sculpture from 1900 to 1979. Currently closed—check out its many satellite sites.

Transamerica Pyramid (▷ 58)
San Francisco's landmark building, 853ft (260m) high and recognized worldwide, has been closed to visitors since September 11, 2001.

Yerba Buena Gardens (▷ 62)
This is the heart of a vibrant, still-evolving SoMa area that mixes museums and arts venues with commercial spaces.

MORE TO SEE	64

555 California Street
Cartoon Art Museum
Children's Creativity Museum
Chinatown
Chinese Culture Center
Glide Memorial Church

Maiden Lane
Museum of the African Diaspora (MoAD)
Nob Hill
Old St. Mary's Cathedral
Wells Fargo Museum

CITY TOURS

Western Addition to the Mission

Explore beyond San Francisco's high-profile sights and you'll be rewarded in these neighborhoods; home to diverse cultures, eye-catching murals, a beaux-arts masterpiece, a vast collection of Asian art and contrasts in places of worship.

Morning

Start the day in **Japantown** (▷ 46–47) exploring the Japan Center (▷ 124–125)—stores here sell everything from hard-to-find Japanese food to books and samurai swords. Then stop by the **National Japanese American Historical Society** (▷ 72), which features exhibits relating to the Japanese-American experience, and take a look at several churches in the area that are significant for their Japanese-style architecture.

Mid-Morning

Wander into the Civic Center's most beautiful building: the French baroque-styled **City Hall** (▷ 22–23). Tours are offered several times a day, but you can also ascend the grand staircase on your own and look around. Nearby is the **Asian Art Museum** (▷ 66), which has an immense collection spanning 6,000 years and diverse cultures and religions.

Lunch

From the Civic Center area it's a short walk over to **Hayes Valley** (▷ 70), a neighborhood that has undergone a transformation in the last two decades. Hayes Street, the main artery, is lined with interesting shops and restaurants—you can find casual cafés, burgers, pizza and more. **La Boulange de Hayes**, an outpost of La Boulange, a chain of popular French boulangeries, serves sandwiches, salads, brunch items and pastries (500 Hayes Street; daily 7–7).

Afternoon
Walk to **Alamo Square** (▷ 66) from the Hayes Valley shopping area, though be warned that the hill requires a bit of energy. You'll be rewarded at the top with the view of six famous Victorian homes known as the "painted ladies." You can also see the dome of City Hall, the Transamerica Pyramid and other sights from this perch.

Mid-Afternoon
Spend the rest of the afternoon in the **Mission District** (▷ 71–72), where you can explore **Mission Dolores** (▷ 50–51), an adobe building completed in 1791. Mass is still held in the chapel, and also in the neighboring basilica, completed in 1918. Balmy Alley, between 24th and 25th streets, has the area's best murals. For a tour of these and other murals in the area, contact Precita Eyes Mural Center (▷ 71–72).

CITY TOURS

Dinner
The Mission is one of the best restaurant neighborhoods in the city. You won't be disappointed with the Italian fare at **Delfina** (▷ 144), but you're also unlikely to go wrong if you stumble on a place that looks busy and inviting. The neighborhood accommodates all price points and ethnic hankerings.

Evening
Nightlife is also lively in the Mission, where there's live music, clubs and countless bars, or you can see who's performing at **The Independent** (▷ 135), in the Western Addition. For cultural activities like the ballet, symphony and opera—held at Civic Center venues like **Louise M. Davies Symphony Hall** (▷ 135) and the **War Memorial Opera House** (▷ 137)—you'll have to plan ahead and buy tickets in advance.

JAPANTOWN

National Japanese American Historical Society

Peace Pagoda

Sutter Street
Post Street
GOUGH

BOULEVARD

GEARY

Cleary Court

St Mary's Cathedral

Ellis

O'Farrell Street

Steiner Street

Fillmore Street

Hollis Street

Willow Street

Laguna Street

Eddy

Jefferson Square

Turk

St John Coltrane African Orthodox Church

ANZA VISTA Street

Ellis Street

Eddy Street

Golden Gate

McAllister

Turk

Golden Gate Avenue

Broderick Street

Scott Street

Pierce Street

Steiner Street

VAN NESS CIVIC CENTER

WESTERN ADDITION

Fulton

Baker Street

Fulton

Broderick Street

DIVISADERO Street

Street

African American Art & Culture Complex

Octavia Street

Grove

Ivy Street

Boulevard

Alamo Square

HAYES VALLEY

La Boulange de Hayes

Grove

The Independent

Hayes Street

ALAMO SQUARE

FELL Street

Hickory Street

OAK Street

FELL

OAK STREET

Broderick Street

Scott Street

Pierce Street

Steiner Street

Fillmore

Webster Street

Buchanan Street

Laguna Street

Octavia Blvd

Page Street

Koshland Park

Haight Street

Page Street

Haight

Waller Street

Hermann Street

Pearl Street

Buena Vista Park

Divisadero Street

Buena Vista Avenue East

Duboce Park

Duboce Park

Duboce Avenue

Duboce / Church

DUBOCE

Buena Vista Avenue

Castro Street

Noe Street

Walter Street

Sanchez Street

Belcher Street

Church Street

DOLORES STREET

GUERRERO STREET

14th Street

Ramona Street

Corona Heights Park

Randall Museum

Museum Way

Flint Street

Henry Street

14th Street

Church Street

15th Street

Landers Street

15th Street

Beaver Street

MARKET STREET

MISSION DOLORES

States Street

Castro

17TH STREET

MARKET STREET

16TH STREET

Pond Street

Prosper Street

Church Street

Mission Dolores

DOLORES STREET

17th Street

Ford Street

CASTRO

18th Street

18TH STREET

Hancock Street

Church / 18th

Mission Dolores Park

Delfina

19th Street

K

L

M

5

6

7

8

9

Western Addition to the Mission
Quick Reference Guide

City Hall (▷ 22)

This beaux-arts masterpiece has a black-and-gold copper dome that can be seen from many points around the city. Inside, the grand staircase is lined with wrought-iron banisters and illuminated by free-standing and hanging lamps. The building was completed in 1915 at a cost of $3.5 million. The aim of the authorities was to show San Francisco's superiority over the city of Los Angeles.

Japantown (▷ 46)

San Francisco's Japanese-American community, the first in the United States, once spanned 30 blocks of the Western Addition. Today Japantown's commercial hub is the large Japan Center (two indoor malls connected by a plaza), while several churches in the area feature Japanese-style architecture. Other highlights include the National Japanese American Historical Society.

Mission Dolores (▷ 50)

Part of a chain of 21 missions built in California by the Spanish, Mission Dolores is the oldest building in the city. Its thick adobe walls helped the structure withstand several earthquakes. Headstones in the cemetery mark Spanish- and Mexican-era notables. The mission's tiny yet atmospheric chapel has an altar dating from 1780, as well as frescoes by Native Americans.

Golden Gate Park

One of the world's largest urban parks, Golden Gate Park stretches from the middle of the city to the ocean, encompassing outstanding museums, gardens, lakes, a golf course and windmills. Nearby is the freethinking Haight–Ashbury, birthplace of 1967's Summer of Love.

Morning
You could spend all day walking around **Golden Gate Park** (▷ 38–39), but start your exploration at one of a trio of lovely gardens, all located in the eastern section of the park: the **Conservatory of Flowers** (▷ 68), the **Japanese Tea Garden** (▷ 70–71) and the **San Francisco Botanical Garden at Strybing Arboretum** (▷ 74). Nature lovers will appreciate the incredible variety of plants and flowers on view from around the globe at any one of these sights.

Mid-Morning
Two very different but impressive museums are just a short walk from each other, so choose which one you'd like to visit: The **de Young** (▷ 28–29) is an art museum that also plays host to first-rate traveling exhibitions; the **California Academy of Sciences** (▷ 18–19) covers everything from the land and sea to the outer reaches of the solar system—there are a number of exhibits and activities that will entertain children, including the state-of-the-art Morrison Planetarium.

Lunch
Both museums have solid dining choices, so stick around for lunch. The **de Young's café** has outdoor seating by its sculpture garden, while the California Academy of Sciences has highly regarded chefs behind its restaurant (**Moss Room**) and its more casual **café**.

Afternoon

Explore more of **Golden Gate Park**. Activities include a boat ride on Stow Lake and a carousel ride for kids, or take advantage of one of the park's 21 tennis courts (lessons are available, too). Then take a short detour north of the park to explore the **Columbarium** (▷ 68), a Victorian structure that houses ashes of the deceased. While it might sound morbid, it's quintessentially San Francisco (though many locals don't even know it exists). Arrange a tour, if possible—almost every niche has a fascinating story.

Mid-Afternoon

Wander down historic Haight Street, in **Haight–Ashbury** (▷ 42–43). The area's hippie, Summer-of-Love reputation has shifted over the years and yuppies might now trump deadheads (followers of the band the Grateful Dead). But the area still bears some vestiges of its Grateful Dead roots, with shops selling tie-dye shirts, pipes and other deadhead gear. Other stores sell funky, contemporary clothes and shoes.

Dinner

Stay in the Haight–Ashbury area for dinner and nightlife. At a spot like **Alembic** (▷ 132), you can have both in one location. After dinner, find out what's playing at the **Red Vic** (1727 Haight Street), an independent movie theater showing a mix of recent and old films. Note that it's wise to steer clear of Golden Gate Park after dark—as with any park, there are many isolated areas that aren't safe at night.

0 500 m
0 500 yds

Presidio

Golden Gate National Recreation Area

Baker Beach

China Beach

Sea Cliff Avenue

James D Phelan State Park

Scenic Way

Camino Del Mar

SEA CLIFF

West Clay Street

LAKE STREET

Lake Street

Mountain Lake

California Street

Sutro Annex Park

Clement Street

Tacoma Street

GEARY BOULEVARD

CENTRAL RICHMOND

Anza Street

Balboa Street

Cabrillo Avenue

FULTON STREET

PARK PRESIDIO BOULEVARD

CROSSOVER DRIVE

de Young Museum

John F Kennedy Drive

Marx Meadow

Lloyd Lake

Lindley Meadow

Golden Gate Park Stadium

Overlook Drive

Middle Drive West

Elk Glen Lake

Metson Lake

Mallard Lake

Golden Gate Park

Japanese Tea Garden

Strawberry Hill

Stow Lake

San Francisco Botanical Garden at Strybing Arboretum

Martin Luther King Junior Drive

LINCOLN WAY

Irving Street

CENTRAL SUNSET

Judah / 19th Avenue

INNER SUNSET

Judah Street

Kirkham Street

Lawton Street

BOULEVARD

Stilwell Road

Pershing Drive

LINCOLN BOULEVARD

Baker Court

Wedemeyer Street

Haas Street

PARK PRESIDIO BOULEVARD

Funston Avenue

Golden Gate Park Quick Reference Guide

SIGHTS AND EXPERIENCES

California Academy of Sciences (▷ 18)

Pritzker Prize-winning architect Renzo Piano designed this "green" museum, creating a living roof that houses a state-of-the-art planetarium, an aquarium, natural history museum and rainforest dome, where the temperature reaches a warming 85°F (29°C).

de Young Museum (▷ 28)

Damage to the de Young Museum from the 1989 Loma Prieta earthquake led to a stunning new building in Golden Gate Park, unveiled in 2005. The permanent collection focuses on American painting and decorative arts; the 144ft (44m) observation tower is a highlight.

Golden Gate Park (▷ 38)

Modeled after New York's Central Park, this vast, 1,000-acre (405ha) urban park is home to museums, gardens, lakes, windmills, a golf course and more; it also hosts festivals and special events throughout the year and it's popular with joggers, kite-fliers and roller-skaters.

Haight–Ashbury (▷ 42)

Holding hundreds of elegant Victorian homes that survived the 1906 earthquake, and becoming world-famous as the heart of hippiedom in 1967, Haight–Ashbury still means Peace and Love to many people. It has vintage clothing outlets and bookstores and is a center for alternative lifestyles.

Eye-catching decoration on a house in Haight–Ashbury

Enjoying the Japanese Tea Garden

Farther Afield

If you have a bit more time in the Bay Area, explore a few neighborhoods and state parks that are slightly off the tourist path, but worth investigating. Also incorporate a trip across the Bay Bridge to Berkeley and Oakland, where the weather warms up and the fog lifts, but the character remains.

DAY 1
Morning
Spend your morning in the East Bay, starting with the **UC Berkeley Campus** (▷ 60–61). Amble down Telegraph Avenue, the main drag on the south side of campus, and walk through Sather Gate to see Sproul Plaza, where the 1960s Free Speech Movement was born. The Campanile is also a highlight.

Lunch
Don't miss the opportunity to try **Chez Panisse** café (1517 Shattuck Avenue, Berkeley; Mon–Sat 9–9.30), helmed by influential chef Alice Waters, who has been a proponent of local, seasonal ingredients for decades. Her formal restaurant downstairs is open for dinner only, but her upstairs café is less expensive and open for lunch.

Afternoon
After lunch, visit the **Oakland Museum of California** (▷ 52–53), which provides lively, informative exhibits about the ever-evolving art, history and nature of California. Its garden has lovely views of Lake Merritt.

Dinner
Go to the Berkeley/Oakland border to dine at **Wood Tavern** (6317 College Avenue, Oakland; daily lunch and dinner), a neighborhood restaurant serving California-Mediterranean cuisine on College Avenue. The street also has other good dining options, a movie theater, cafés and bars.

DAY 2
Morning
Start your day exploring two side-by-side neighborhoods with different personalities: **Noe Valley** (▷ 75) and the **Castro** (▷ 75). The heart of commercial Noe Valley is 24th Street, where you'll share the sidewalk with strollers (pushchairs) and dogs as you peruse the inviting shops. Then head over to the Castro, San Francisco's famous gay district, where politician and gay-rights activist Harvey Milk opened his camera shop and launched a movement. Most of the action is on Castro Street between Market and 19th streets; the famous **Castro Theatre** (▷ 133) is on Castro and Market.

Lunch
Make your way across town to the **Fort Mason Center** (▷ 69) and **Greens** (▷ 145), a vegetarian restaurant where even meat-lovers won't miss a thing, especially with the views of the Golden Gate Bridge and the San Francisco Bay.

Afternoon
From Fort Mason, walk over to Fisherman's Wharf and take a scenic ferry ride to **Angel Island State Park** (▷ 75), which is the largest island in the Bay (though not as famous as Alcatraz, its neighbor). Angel Island has hiking trails and bike paths to keep you occupied for several hours.

Evening
Take the ferry back to Fisherman's Wharf and ride the cable car up steep Hyde Street to **Zarzuela** (▷ 149), a Russian Hill restaurant serving tapas, sangria and other traditional Spanish dishes. After dinner, walk down to Polk Street for a nightcap.

Sonoma Valley

SAN RAFAEL

San Pablo
Bay

KENTFIELD

San Rafael
Bay

GREENBRAE

SAN
QUENTIN

580

RICHMOND-SAN RAFAEL BRIDGE

CORTE MADERA

101

Mount
Tamalpais
State Park

MILL VALLEY

STRAWBERRY POINT

Muir Woods
National
Monument

TIBURON

BELVEDERE

MARIN CITY

Muir
Beach

Golden Gate
National
Recreation
Area

101

SAUSALITO

Angel Island
State Park

Alcatraz
Island

GOLDEN GATE
BRIDGE

PRESIDIO

Presidio
National
Park

101

Lincoln
Park

San Francisco
Caltrain Station

SAN FRANCISCO

Golden Gate Park

CASTRO

280

OCEAN
BEACH

NOE
VALLEY

San Francisco
Zoo

PACIFIC

Lake
Merced

280

101

OCEAN

35

DALY
CITY

San Bruno Mountain
State & County Park

BROADMOOR

COLMA

Brisbane

Mussel
Rock
Park

82

SOUTH
SAN FRANCISCO

280

PACIFICA

380

82

101

SAN BRUNO

San Jose

Stanford
University

SAN
PABLO

RICHMOND

80

Wildcat
Canyon
Regional Park

San Pablo
Reservoir

Briones
Regional
Park

EL CERRITO

123

Briones
Reservoir

KENSINGTON

ALBANY

Tilden
Regional Park

580/80

BERKELEY

ORINDA

UC Berkeley
Campus

24

13

123

Treasure
Island

24

EMERYVILLE

SAN FRANCISCO - OAKLAND BAY BRIDGE

80

PIEDMONT

Redwood
Regional
Park

980

13

580

OAKLAND

880

Oakland Museum
of California

China
Basin

61

580

Alameda

185

SAN
LEANDRO

Bay Farm
Island

880

Oakland
International
Airport

SAN
LORENZO

San Francisco Bay

0   5 km
0   3 miles

San Francisco
International
Airport

SAN MATEO-HAYWARD BRIDGE

92

Farther Afield Quick Reference Guide

★ SIGHTS AND EXPERIENCES
TOP 25

Oakland Museum of California
(▷ 52)
This East Bay museum leads the way in documenting the history, nature and art of the Golden State. An extensive renovation, which has recently been completed, has added a spring to the museum's step; it's now a much more interactive, entertaining place.

UC Berkeley Campus (▷ 60)
Museums, libraries and architecturally distinguished buildings draw visitors to this campus, once a hotbed of political dissent. The first of 10 University of California campuses, highlights for visitors include the Berkeley Art Museum, elegant Sather Gate and the Campanile.

CITY TOURS

MORE TO SEE	64

Angel Island State Park
Castro
Noe Valley
San Francisco Zoo

San Jose
Sausalito
Sonoma Valley
Stanford University

SHOP	118

Clothes
Wild Card

Offbeat
Global Exchange

ENTERTAINMENT	128

Bars and Cafés
Café Flore

Movie Theaters
Castro Theatre

EAT	138

Asian
Eric's Restaurant

Shop

Whether you're looking for the best local products, a department store or a quirky boutique, you'll find them all in San Francisco. In this section shops are listed alphabetically.

SHOP

Introduction

While San Francisco may not be in the same shopping league as London, Paris or New York, many prefer its slower pace and are surprised by the array of paraphernalia to be found. Each neighborhood reflects its style in the clothes, furnishings, antiques, books, food and souvenirs on offer, making shopping an enjoyable accompaniment to exploring these different areas.

A Memento of Your Visit

Various knick-knacks decorated with the Golden Gate Bridge, Alcatraz or the words "I Left My Heart in San Francisco" predominate among the souvenirs widely found in Fisherman's Wharf and the smaller sprinkling of trinket outlets in Chinatown and downtown. Those of a nervous disposition might choose to avoid the many jokey earthquake-related items, while Ghirardelli chocolate makes a good gift for anyone with a sweet tooth. The produce of California's numerous wineries is stocked throughout the city. Having chosen your wine, head to the local bakery for a loaf of Boudin's sourdough bread (▷ 143). The Boudin tradition continues with the same distinctive sourdough that arrived in San Francisco during the Gold Rush. A local specialty is fresh clam chowder served in a sourdough bread bowl.

Something Unique

In Chinatown and the less-tourist-visited Asian shops on Clement Street in the Richmond District are rich pickings for amateur cooks

---

MUSEUM STORES

Unique jewellery, sustainable gifts, clothing and accessories and books and toys with a nature theme are all on sale at The California Academy of Sciences' museum shop. The Exploratorium has nature and science books and quirky science-related items including kits about weather, solar power and rainbow crystals.

Clockwise from top: Shop signs in Haight–Ashbury; food and drink at Molinari Deli, in the Italian District; bags for sale in a store in Fillmore Street; pink lilies

looking to extend their stocks of utensils or to select from an array of otherwise hard-to-find spices and herbs.

Vintage San Francisco

Rich with new and secondhand bookstores, San Francisco was a fulcrum of the 1950s Beat explosion and is the best place to find the definitive stock of Beat and Beat-related literature and criticism. Haight–Ashbury's original hippies may have moved on but the tie-dyed T-shirts and other totems of flower power are still available along Haight Street, which is also the best stop in the city for wacky, vintage clothing and obscure CDs and vinyl.

Other Shopping Districts

Other noted neighborhood shopping streets include Chestnut Street in the Marina District, Union and Fillmore streets in Pacific Heights, and Hayes Street in burgeoning Hayes Valley, all proferring generally smart clothing, antiques and household items. In North Beach, Grant Avenue has outlets for bric-a-brac and unusual crafts as well as silks and pearls. The Mission District is now the destination for furniture, funky designers and independent stores.

STYLE OVER SUBSTANCE

"Design matters" proclaimed the San Francisco-based magazine *One*. The publication lasted less than a year, but the slogan is still relevant. Design has always played an important role in San Francisco. The iconic images of the Golden Gate National Recreation Area from graphic designer Michael Schweb are found on posters, mugs, T-shirts and calendars. Furniture is also an art form in some San Francisco stores. HD Buttercup (✉ 290 Townsend Street ☎ 415/820–4788) offers a stylish home furnishings shopping experience, while New Deal (✉ 4529 18th Street ☎ 415/552–6208) has furniture, lighting and artworks to enhance any design-conscious pad.

make a cheerful greeting for customers; Californian wine is a popular purchase; loaves of sourdough bread and tins of clam chowder for sale at Boudin's Bakery

Directory

Pacific Heights to Telegraph Hill

Bookstores
City Lights
National Park Store
Clothes
Heidi Says
Mingle
Revolver
Secondhand Clothes
Cris
Shoes
Gimme Shoes
Shopping Centers
Ghirardelli Square
Pier 39

Downtown to Nob Hill

Art and Antiques
Andrea Schwartz Gallery
Gump's
Hang Art
John Berggruen Gallery
Museumstore
Xanadu Gallery
Bookstores
Crocker Galleria
William Stout Architectural Books
Clothes
Chanel Boutique
The Hound
Metier
Old Vogue
Rolo SoMa
Wilkes Bashford

Cosmetics and Perfumes
Sephora
Discount Outlets
Jeremys
Food and Drink
Ten Ren Tea Company
High-tech
Apple Store
Offbeat
Clarion Music Center
Shopping Centers
Embarcadero Center
Westfield San Francisco

Western Addition to the Mission

Art and Antiques
Zonal
Clothes
Dema
Discount Outlets
Crossroads Trading Co.
Thrift Town
Offbeat
Needles & Pens
Secondhand Clothes
Ver Unica
Shopping Centers
Japan Center

Farther Afield

Clothes
Wild Card
Offbeat
Global Exchange

SHOP

Shopping A–Z

ANDREA SCHWARTZ GALLERY
www.asgallery.com
This large exhibition space is devoted to contemporary painting, installations and mixed media.
✚ R6 ✉ 545 4th Street ☎ 415/495–2090 🕐 Mon–Fri 9–5, Sat 1–5
🚌 8, 47

APPLE STORE
www.apple.com/retail/sanfrancisco
Where better to sample Apple's latest innovations? Expect product demos and a buzzing atmosphere.
✚ Q5 ✉ 1 Stockton Street ☎ 415/392–0202 🕐 Mon–Sat 9–9, Sun 10–8
🚌 2, 3, 30, 45

CHANEL BOUTIQUE

www.chanel.com

Two floors filled with clothes, cosmetics and much more from the renowned French designer are available for the woman with refined taste.

➕ Q5 ✉ 156 Geary Street ☎ 415/981–1550 🕐 Mon–Sat 10–6, Sun 12–5 🚌 2, 3, 30, 45

CITY LIGHTS

www.citylights.com

City Lights is a publishing company and bookstore, inextricably linked to the 1950s Beat Generation, founded by poet Lawrence Ferlinghetti. The stock includes many of the movement's definitive writings, fiction and nonfiction, and literary magazines.

➕ Q3 ✉ 261 Columbus Avenue ☎ 415/362–8193 🕐 Daily 10am–midnight 🚌 30, 41, 45

CLARION MUSIC CENTER

www.clarionmusic.com

Regulars might rent a violin or cello, but others can content themselves with a stroll along the racks browsing the wonderful Asian musical instruments, which range from Burmese temple bells to Chinese egg rattles.

➕ Q4 ✉ 816 Sacramento Street ☎ 415/391–1317 🕐 Mon–Fri 11–6, Sat 9–5 🚌 30, 45

CRIS

www.crisconsignment.com

Secondhand-clothes store Cris is a welcome surprise for budget-conscious shoppers in the usually expensive Russian Hill neighborhood, with an array of designer names; mostly for women.

➕ N3 ✉ 2056 Polk Street ☎ 415/474–1191 🕐 Mon–Sat 11–6, Sun 12–6 🚌 19

CROCKER GALLERIA

www.thecrockergalleria.com

Designer clothing stores, food shops and snack stands make this small, chic shopping mall in the Financial District ideal for browsing.

➕ Q5 ✉ 50 Post Street ☎ 415/393–1505 🕐 Mon–Fri 10–6, Sat 10–5 🚌 2, 3, 5, 6

CROSSROADS TRADING CO.

www.crossroadstrading.com

Here you'll find secondhand and discounted new clothes and jewelry, with a youthful bias.

➕ L5 ✉ 1901 Fillmore Street ☎ 415/775–8885 🕐 Mon–Sat 11–8, Sun 11–7 🚌 2, 3, 4, 22, 76

DEMA

www.godemago.com

Stylish stores line Valencia Street, including this shop, with women's designs from owner Dema Grim.

➕ M9 ✉ 1038 Valencia Street ☎ 415/206–0500 🕐 Mon–Fri 11–7, Sat 12–7, Sun 12–6 🚇 24th Street–Mission 🚌 14, 49

SHOP

EMBARCADERO CENTER

www.embarcaderocenter.com

Pick up a free map to plot a course around the walkways, plazas and stores of this three-level shopping complex spanning eight city blocks.

🚩 R4 ✉ Battery Street, between Clay and Sacramento streets ☎ 415/772–0700 🕐 Mon–Fri 10–7, Sat 10–6, Sun 12–5 🚌 1, 41

GHIRARDELLI SQUARE

▷ 69.

GIMME SHOES

www.gimmeshoes.com

This store sells shoes by a range of designers, from Sigerson Morrison to Adidas.

🚩 L4 ✉ 2358 Fillmore Street ☎ 415/441–3040 🕐 Mon–Sat 11–7, Sun 12–6 🚌 1, 22

GLOBAL EXCHANGE

www.globalexchangestore.com

The store of a human rights organization sells clothing, artworks and more from the Third World, guaranteed not to be produced in sweatshops or in environmentally destructive ways.

🚩 Off map at L9 ✉ 4018 24th Street ☎ 415/648–8068 🕐 Mon, Sun 11–6, Tue–Fri 11–7, Sat 10–7 🚇 16th Street–Mission 🚌 37, 48

GUMP'S

www.gumps.com

Gump's has been held in high esteem since 1861 and sells antiques from all over the world, particularly Asia. An art gallery specializes in works by emergent artists and another room is devoted to jade.

🚩 Q5 ✉ 135 Post Street ☎ 415/982–1616 🕐 Mon–Sat 10–6, Sun 12–5 🚌 2, 3, 76

HANG ART

www.hangart.com

Hang Art displays what it believes is the cream of the new crop of Bay Area artists.

🚩 P5 ✉ 567 Sutter Street ☎ 415/434–4264 🕐 Mon–Sat 10–6, Sun 12–5 🚌 1, 3, 38

HEIDI SAYS

www.heidisays.com

This Pacific Heights boutique has clothes, shoes and accessories from new and established designers. Heidi Says Casual is two doors down, and Heidi Says Shoes is down the street (2105 Fillmore).

🚩 L4 ✉ 2426 Fillmore Street ☎ 415/749–0655 🕐 Mon–Sat 11–7, Sun 12–6 🚌 1, 22

THE HOUND

www.thehound.com

The Hound offers expensive, high-quality menswear, much of it based on popular perceptions of what an English country gentleman likes to wear.

🚩 Q4 ✉ 140 Sutter Street ☎ 415/989–0429 🕐 Mon–Fri 9.30–6, Sat 9.30–5.30 🚌 2, 3, 76

JAPAN CENTER

From kimonos to rice cookers to samurai swords, Japanese arts and crafts are well represented in this complex of stores, restaurants and offices.

🚇 L5–M5 ✉ Post Street, between Laguna and Fillmore streets ☎ No phone 🕐 Store and restaurant hours vary 🚌 2, 3, 38

JEREMYS

www.jeremys.com

A wide selection of discounted men's and women's clothing is sold here, often from high-end designers and department stores. Be aware that some items have slight defects.

🚇 R6 ✉ 2 South Park ☎ 415/882–4929 🕐 Mon–Wed, Fri–Sat 11–6, Thu 11–8, Sun 12–6 🚌 10

JOHN BERGGRUEN GALLERY

www.berggruen.com

Some of the leading names of 20th-century American art are to be found through the three floors of this highly regarded gallery, which also features selected European works.

🚇 Q5 ✉ 228 Grant Avenue ☎ 415/781–4629 🕐 Mon–Fri 9.30–5.30, Sat 10.30–5 🚌 2, 3, 76

METIER

www.metiersf.com

This understated boutique just off Union Square carries a wide range of high-quality jewelry and accessories from the likes of Alexander Wang, 3.1 Phillip Lim and Vanessa Bruno.

🚇 Q5 ✉ 210 Post Street ☎ 415/590–2998 🕐 Mon, Thu–Sat 12–6 🚌 2, 38, 56

MINGLE

www.mingleshop.com

Designers and artists rotate frequently at this boutique selling clothes, jewelry, accessories and art. New items, often one-of-a-kind, enter the mix weekly.

🚇 M3 ✉ 1815 Union Street ☎ 415/674–8811 🕐 Wed–Mon 11–7 🚌 41, 45

MUSEUMSTORE

http://museumstore.sfmoma.org

The store of the San Francisco Museum of Modern Art sells an exemplary collection of art-related books, posters and souvenirs.

🚇 Q5 ✉ San Francisco Museum of Modern Art, 151 3rd Street ☎ 888/357–0037 🕐 Mon–Wed, Fri–Sun 10–6.30, Thu 10–9.30 🚌 12, 30, 45, 76

NATIONAL PARK STORE

http://store.parksconservancy.org

Browse here for books, magazines and videos devoted to wild California and the natural history of the American West.

🚇 P1 ✉ Pier 39, Fisherman's Wharf ☎ 415/433–7221 🕐 Sun–Thu 10–9, Fri–Sat 10–9.30 🚌 10, 19, 47

ONE-STOP SHOPPING

Shoppers will discover many major department stores within walking distance of each other, either in the Union Square area or in Westfield San Francisco shopping center. Neiman Marcus (✉ 150 Stockton Street ☎ 415/362–3900), Saks Fifth Avenue (✉ 220 Post Street ☎ 415/986–4300), Bloomingdale's (✉ Westfield San Francisco, 865 Market Street ☎ 415/856–5720) and Barneys New York (✉ 77 O'Farrell Street ☎ 415/268–3500) compete for attention from bigger spenders, while Macy's West (✉ 170 O'Farrell Street ☎ 415/397–3333) and Nordstrom (✉ Westfield San Francisco, 865 Market Street ☎ 415/243–8500) have quality merchandise at more affordable prices.

NEEDLES & PENS
www.needles-pens.com
Needles & Pens sells clothes and other exclusive creations from local artists, plus a vast stock of off-beat magazines and local magazines published on a shoestring.
➕ M8 ✉ 3252 16th Street ☎ 415/255–1534 🕐 Daily 12–7 🚇 16th Street–Mission 🚌 14, 49

OLD VOGUE
At Old Vogue you can find a great selection of vintage men's clothing. Look out for the array of high quality cashmere jumpers and leather jackets in particular.
➕ Q3 ✉ 1412 Grant Avenue ☎ 415/392–1522 🕐 Tue–Sat 12–6 🚌 39

PIER 39
www.pier39.com
With 100 or more stores to choose from, visitors to Pier 39 can find San Francisco souvenirs to take home, magic kits, crazy hats and more. Don't miss the sunbathing sea lions.
➕ P1 ✉ Pier 39, Fisherman's Wharf 🕐 Daily 10–9 🚌 8X, 39, 47, F

There's plenty of choice at Pier 39

REVOLVER
www.revolveronline.com
Revolver is known for its beautiful, high quality men's and women's clothing and accessories. It is worthwhile checking out the website before you visit.
➕ L4 ✉ 136 Fillmore Street ☎ 415/779–2712 🕐 Daily 12–8 🚌 6, 22, 71

SEPHORA
www.sephora.com
A visual explosion of color accompanies high-end cosmetics and fragrances from companies such as Stila and Christian Dior.
➕ P5 ✉ 33 Powell Street ☎ 415/362–9360 🕐 Mon–Sat 10–9, Sun 10–7 🚇 Powell Street 🚌 30, 45

TEN REN TEA COMPANY
www.tenren.com
This Chinatown store is packed with more than 40 blends from around the world. You can taste before you buy.
➕ Q4 ✉ 949 Grant Avenue ☎ 415/362–0656 🕐 Mon–Sat 9–9 🚌 30, 41

THRIFT TOWN
www.thrifttown.com
Packed from floor to ceiling with donated secondhand clothing, furniture, books and lots more, this is one of the largest of San Francisco's thrift stores. Many others are listed in the phone book.
➕ N9 ✉ 2101 Mission Street ☎ 415/861–1132 🕐 Mon–Fri 9–9, Sat 10–7, Sun 10–6 🚇 16th Street–Mission 🚌 14, 49

VER UNICA
www.verunicasf.com
Ver Unica has a mighty stock of vintage wear, for both men and

women, plus shoes, handbags and assorted accessories.

🚼 M6 ✉ 437B Hayes Street ☎ 415/431–0688 🕐 Mon–Sat 11–7, Sun 12–6 🚌 21

WESTFIELD SAN FRANCISCO

http://westfield.com/sanfrancisco
Nordstrom and Bloomingdale's department stores anchor this large indoor shopping center.

🚼 Q5 ✉ 865 Market Street ☎ 415/512–6776 🕐 Mon–Sat 10–8.30, Sun 10–7 🚃 Powell Street 🚌 5, 6, 9, 21, 31, 71

WILKES BASHFORD

www.wilkesbashford.com
You'll find classy men's and women's clothing across six impressively well-stocked floors here.

🚼 Q4 ✉ 375 Sutter Street ☎ 415/986–4380 🕐 Mon–Sat 10–6 🚌 2, 3, 30, 45, 76

WILLIAM STOUT ARCHITECTURAL BOOKS

www.stoutbooks.com
A range of architectural tomes in sufficient quantity to attract both the professional architect and the interested amateur are stocked at this store.

🚼 Q3 ✉ 804 Montgomery Street ☎ 415/391–6757 🕐 Mon–Fri 10–6.30, Sat 10–5.30 🚌 41

WILD CARD

This fun shop has one of the city's best card selections and plenty of novelties, souvenirs and gay accessories.

🚼 L9 ✉ 3989 17th Street ☎ 415/626–4449 🕐 Daily 11–8 🚌 24, 35, 37

XANADU GALLERY

www.xanadugallery.us
Browse Xanadu Gallery for highly decorative items created

from amber gathered in northern California, as well as a range of handicrafts and jewelry from Africa and Asia.

🚼 Q5 ✉ 140 Maiden Lane ☎ 415/392–9999 🕐 Tue–Sat 10–6 🚌 2, 3, 41, 30, 45

ZONAL

www.zonalhome.com
Antique furniture, contemporary furnishings and other attention-grabbing collectibles make this store perfect for browsing.

🚼 M6 ✉ 568 Hayes Street ☎ 415/255–9307 🕐 Tue–Sat 11–6, Sun 12–5 🚌 21

A store in Chinatown

SHOP

127

Entertainment

Once you've done with sightseeing for the day, you'll find lots of other great things to do with your time in this chapter, even if all you want to do is relax with a drink. In this section establishments are listed alphabetically.

ENTERTAINMENT

Introduction

Late-opening stores, restaurants, bars and spectacular views all enliven San Francisco after dark. Prime evening areas include North Beach, the Mission District and the Marina. The Union Square area is the hub for theater, SoMa has the latest nightclubs, while evening activities at Fisherman's Wharf are geared toward tourists, and often families.

Drinks with a View

San Francisco's topography lends itself to stunning views, and many hotels, in particular, take advantage of this. You can relax with a cocktail as you take in the view from Harry Denton's Starlight Room on the 21st floor of the Sir Francis Drake Hotel (450 Powell Street). Alternatively, have a drink in swanky Nob Hill at the Top of the Mark, a lounge on the 19th floor of the InterContinental Mark Hopkins (999 California Street) with sweeping views of the city. It offers a menu of 100 martinis, food service all day, plus afternoon tea. Or try the Marriott Hotel's 39th-floor lounge, The View (55 Fourth Street), from which it's an easy walk to SoMa or Union Square for dinner.

High-end Cocktails

Though the wine bar craze continues in San Francisco, another trend is the prevalence of the high-end cocktail: top shelf ingredients, innovative combinations and expert preparation. Many bartenders, now sometimes called "mixologists," have elevated the cocktail to an art form. The upside can be a fantastic and

---

UP, UP AND AWAY

For a truly spectacular city adventure, take an urban helicopter flight. San Francisco Helicopter Tours (☎ 415/515–5400) offers a package that includes a flight, followed by dinner and dancing aboard the *Hornblower* yacht as it sails around the Bay.

Clockwise from top: Grant Avenue, in Chinatown, lit up at night; clubs abound in San Francisco; start the evening with a top-notch cocktail; neon lights illuminate

unusual drink—or a new spin on a classic. The downside can be a longer wait at the bar. If you fancy a delicious cocktail, stop by Rickhouse (246 Kearny Street), have drinks and dinner at Beretta (▷ 142) or Bar Agricole (355 11th Street), or make a reservation at Bourbon & Branch (▷ 133), a former Prohibition-era speakeasy.

Laughs, Games and More

In addition to the city's varied bars and clubs, there are also several places to go for a good laugh. Cobb's (▷ 134) and Punch Line (▷ 136) draw nationally known comedians, while BATS Improv (▷ 133) is a terrific destination for comedy on the fly. Family fun includes the Presidio Bowl (at the corner of Moraga and Montgomery), a 12-lane bowling alley in the lovely Presidio, and the arcade at the Metreon (▷ 136). The city also has movie theaters showing independent and mainstream films.

Logistics

Most clubs and bars open nightly, from around 9pm, but are busiest around midnight, closing at 2am (some clubs stay open later, though they can't serve alcohol). Last call for many bars is about 30 minutes before closing time. While clubs in New York and Los Angeles often have a line outside waiting to get in, that typically happens only at the hottest new spots in San Francisco. Music venues generally open 45 minutes to an hour before show time.

BREWERY TOUR

To learn more about the drinks you consume in the evening, spend a few daylight hours at Anchor Brewing Company. The Potrero Hill brewery offers two free tours every weekday (reservations essential ☎ 415/863–8350; www.anchorbrewing.com), followed by a tasting session.

---

the street scene; the Transamerica Pyramid and the Sentinel Building at dusk

Directory

Pacific Heights to Telegraph Hill

Bars and Cafés
Buena Vista Café
Ottimista Enoteca Café
Tosca Café
Clubs/Music
Bimbo's 365 Club
Lou's Pier 47
Comedy
BATS Improv
Cobb's
Movie Theaters
Clay Theatre
Theaters
Club Fugazi
Magic Theatre

Downtown to Nob Hill

Arts Centers
Yerba Buena Center for the Arts
Bars and Cafés
Bourbon & Branch
District
House of Shields
Tonga Room
Clubs/Music
The Endup
Comedy
Punch Line
Movie Theaters
Metreon
Theaters
American Conservatory Theater
Curran Theatre

Western Addition to the Mission

Bars and Cafés
El Techno de Lolinda
Orbit Room
Clubs/Music
Boom Boom Room
Café du Nord
Elbo Room
The Fillmore
Great American Music Hall
The Independent
Slim's
Yoshi's
Concert Halls
Louise M. Davies Symphony Hall
War Memorial Opera House
Movie Theaters
Sundance Kabuki Cinema
Theaters
Herbst Theatre
Theater Rhinoceros

Golden Gate Park

Bars and Cafés
Alembic
Toronado

Farther Afield

Bars and Cafés
Café Flore
Movie Theaters
Castro Theatre

Entertainment A–Z

ALEMBIC
www.alembicbar.com
Enjoy unusual cocktails, fine beers and first-rate small plates at this chic hangout in Upper Haight.
🚩 J7 ✉ 1725 Haight Street ☎ 415/666–0822 🕐 Daily noon–2am
🚌 71, N–Judah

AMERICAN CONSERVATORY THEATER
www.act-sf.org
The highly professional and thought-provoking productions here are well regarded.
🚩 P5 ✉ 415 Geary Street ☎ 415/749–2228 🚌 38

BATS IMPROV

www.improv.org

Innovative improvised theater in Fort Mason (▷ 69) has been making audiences laugh for more than 25 years.

➕ L2 ✉ B350 Fort Mason Center, Marina Boulevard at Laguna Street ☎ 415/474–6776 🚌 22, 28, 30, 49

BIMBO'S 365 CLUB

www.bimbos365club.com

Drawing crowds since 1931, this spacious North Beach club entertains with swingers, crooners and the occasional rocker.

➕ P2 ✉ 1025 Columbus Avenue ☎ 415/474–0365 🕐 Hours vary 🚌 30; Powell–Hyde cable car

BOOM BOOM ROOM

www.boomboomblues.com

No-frills funk, jazz and blues are performed by local and national artists at this Fillmore Street venue. It was founded by the legendary blues guitarist John Lee Hooker.

➕ L5 ✉ 1601 Fillmore Street ☎ 415/673–8000 🕐 Tue–Thu 4pm–12am, Fri–Sat 3pm–12am, Sun 4pm–12am 🚌 22, 38

BOURBON & BRANCH

www.bourbonandbranch.com

First-rate spirits and deft bartending are the focus at this former 1920s speakeasy in the Tenderloin (near downtown). Go online to make a reservation and get the password necessary for entry.

➕ P5 ✉ 501 Jones Street ☎ 415/346–1735 🕐 Mon–Sat 6pm–2am 🚌 38

BUENA VISTA CAFÉ

www.thebuenavista.com

This place serves good, inexpensive food in a pricey area. It's known for its punch-packing Irish coffee.

INSIDE CAFÉS

San Francisco is renowned for its proliferation of European-style cafés, found in every neighborhood, and there is no better place to check the pulse of the city. In North Beach, the legendary haunts include Caffe Greco (✉ 423 Columbus ☎ 415/397–6261), Caffe Roma (✉ 526 Columbus ☎ 415/296–7942), Caffe Trieste (✉ 609 Vallejo Street ☎ 415/982–2605) and Vesuvio (✉ 255 Columbus ☎ 415/362–3370), the stomping ground of the original Beats.

➕ N2 ✉ 2765 Hyde Street ☎ 415/474–5044 🕐 Mon–Fri 9am–2am, Sat–Sun 8am–2am 🚌 30; Powell–Hyde cable car

CAFÉ FLORE

http://cafeflore.com

The affectionate nicknames for this spot—such as Café Haircut and Café Bore—reflect its popularity among a mostly gay clientele.

➕ L9 ✉ 2298 Market Street ☎ 415/621–8579 🕐 Tue–Thu, Sun 7am–1am, Fri–Sat 7am–2am 🚌 37, F, J, K, L, M, N

CAFÉ DU NORD

www.cafedunord.com

Hipster San Franciscans quaff cocktails in this basement bar as they listen to blues, jazz and salsa performers.

➕ L8 ✉ 2170 Market Street ☎ 415/861–5016 🚌 37, F

CASTRO THEATRE

www.castrotheatre.com

A decadent 1920s movie palace, complete with Wurlitzer organ, this is an atmospheric setting in which to watch cult, foreign and revival movies.

➕ L9 ✉ 429 Castro Street ☎ 415/621–6120 🚌 24, K, L, M

CLAY THEATRE
www.landmarktheatres.com
The city's oldest continuously running cinema, built in 1910, is a favorite with San Franciscan movie buffs as the main showcase for first-run foreign movies.
➕ L4 ✉ 2261 Fillmore Street
☎ 415/267–4893 🚌 3, 22

CLUB FUGAZI
www.beachblanketbabylon.com
A zany revue, Beach Blanket Babylon, has been running for more than 35 years at this North Beach venue.
➕ P3 ✉ 678 Green Street ☎ 415/421–4222 🚌 30, 41, 45

COBB'S
www.cobbscomedyclub.com
Nationally known names top the bill at this comedy club. Reserve in advance for leading draws.
➕ P2 ✉ 915 Columbus Avenue ☎ 415/928–4320 ⏰ Varies 🚌 30, 41

CURRAN THEATRE
http://shnsf.com/theatres/curran
This is one of several mainstream theaters on Geary Street and is a good choice if you want to see a Broadway blockbuster.
➕ P5 ✉ 445 Geary Street ☎ 415/551–2075 🚌 38

TICKETS
The major ticket agency, Ticketmaster, has numerous outlets at various locations including the TIX booth on Union Square. For a credit card booking or recorded information call ☎ 800/745–3000. TIX offers half-price day-of-performance tickets for Bay Area arts events from a marked booth on the southwest side of Union Square (☎ 415/433–7827).

DISTRICT
www.districtsf.com
In a sleek warehouse-style space, this wine bar has couches, a U-shape bar, dozens of wines by the glass and a lounge menu.
➕ R6 ✉ 216 Townsend Street
☎ 415/896–2120 ⏰ Mon–Fri 4pm–close, Sat 5pm–close 🚌 10, 12, 30, 45

ELBO ROOM
www.elbo.com
Shoot pool downstairs, or pay a small cover for live music upstairs; acts range from Latin salsa to hip-hop to roots.
➕ M9 ✉ 647 Valencia Street
☎ 415/552–7788 🚇 16th Street–Mission
⏰ Daily 5pm–2am 🚌 14, 49

EL TECHO DE LOLINDA
www.eltechosf.com
Great meeting place with city views from a rooftop bar where authentic Latin American street food and brunch with cocktails are served. Look out for special events.
➕ Off map ✉ 2518 Mission Street
☎ 415/550–6970 ⏰ Mon–Thu 4pm–11pm, Fri 4pm–1am, Sat–Sun 11–1am, Sun 11–11pm 🚇 24th Street–Mission 🚌 14

THE ENDUP
www.theendup.com
This is the biggest and most dependable of a number of gay- and lesbian-oriented nightspots, with riotous dance music.
➕ Q6 ✉ 401 6th Street ☎ 415/646–0999 ⏰ Mon 12pm–4am, Tue, Thu 10pm–4am, Fri 11pm–11am, Sat 10pm–12am 🚌 12, 27

THE FILLMORE
www.thefillmore.com
The legendary venue of the psychedelic era has been revamped

and now showcases Bay Area and internationally known rock bands.
🞣 L5 ✉ 1805 Geary Boulevard ☎ 415/346-6000 🚍 22, 38

GREAT AMERICAN MUSIC HALL
www.slimspresents.com/venue-detail/gamh
See eclectic performers in a lavish setting replete with two bars, a balcony and marble columns.
🞣 N5 ✉ 859 O'Farrell Street ☎ 415/885-0750 🚍 19, 38

HERBST THEATRE
www.sfwmpac.org/herbst/ht_index.html
This venue hosts chamber music, recitals and the City Arts and Lectures series.
🞣 N6 ✉ War Veterans' Building, 401 Van Ness Avenue ☎ 415/392-4400 🚇 Civic Center or Van Ness 🚍 5, 21, 47, 49, 80X

HOUSE OF SHIELDS
www.thehouseofshields.com
One of SF's oldest bars, this unpretentious pub is popular with the post-work crowd. Recently restored, it now serves small bites to eat.
🞣 Q5 ✉ 39 New Montgomery Street ☎ 415/284-9958 🕐 Mon–Fri 2pm–2am, Sat–Sun 3pm–2am 🚇 Montgomery 🚍 14, 30, 45

THE INDEPENDENT
www.theindependentsf.com
This is a comfortable, mid-size venue for mainstream rock, jazz and hip-hop talent.
🞣 K6 ✉ 628 Divisadero Street ☎ 415/771–1421 🚍 21, 24

LOUISE M. DAVIES SYMPHONY HALL
www.sfwmpac.org/symphonyhall/sh_index.html
This venue is home to the San Francisco Symphony orchestra, whose season runs September to June. Summer programs include popular music.
🞣 N6 ✉ 201 Van Ness Avenue ☎ 415/864–6000 🚇 Van Ness or Civic Center 🚍 5, 21, 47, 49, 80X

LOU'S PIER 47
www.lousfishshacksf.com
The top-notch blues performers who appear here Friday to Sunday evenings draw appreciative audiences.
🞣 N2 ✉ 300 Jefferson Street ☎ 415/771–5687 🕐 Mon–Fri 4pm–1am, Sat–Sun noon–1am; restaurant daily 11am–11pm 🚍 30; Powell–Hyde cable car

MAGIC THEATRE
www.magictheatre.org
This small theater has an excellent reputation; productions here range from children's plays through to political satire.
🞣 M2 ✉ Building D, Fort Mason Center ☎ 415/441–8822; information 415/441–8001 🚍 22, 28, 30, 47, 49

sidebar left margin ENTERTAINMENT

SPECTATOR SPORTS

The San Francisco Giants baseball team (http://sanfrancisco.giants.mlb.com) plays at AT&T Park, also known locally as the "Miracle on Third Street," a scenic, 40,000-seat stadium. Eight miles (13km) south of the city, Candlestick Park is the football venue for the San Francisco 49ers (www.49ers.com). Limited numbers of tickets are sold on game days, but it is worth checking online at www.stubhub.com, or you can buy in advance through Ticketmaster (www.ticketmaster.com).

METREON

www.westfield.com/metreon

This five-story behemoth has movie theaters, a giant IMAX screen, an arcade with interactive games and various dining options.
Q5 ✉ 135 4th Street ☎ 415/369–6000 🚌 14, 30, 45, 71

ORBIT ROOM

Floor-to-ceiling windows overlook Market Street at this lounge, with a circular bar, which serves innovative drinks made with painstaking care.
M7 ✉ 1900 Market Street ☎ 415/252–9525 🕐 Mon–Fri 5pm–close, Sat–Sun noon–close 🚌 Any Market Street bus

OTTIMISTA ENOTECA CAFÉ

www.ottimistasf.com

Ottimista has a rotating list of 35–40 wines by the glass and a small seasonal menu.
M3 ✉ 1838 Union Street ☎ 415/674–8400 🕐 Mon–Fri 4pm–12am, Sat 11am–2am, Sun 11am–12am 🚌 41, 45

PUNCH LINE

www.punchlinecomedyclub.com

This long-running venue for both aspiring and nationally known comedians has a good record of giving future stars their early break.
Q4 ✉ 444 Battery Street ☎ 415/397–7573 🚌 3, 41

SLIM'S

www.slims-sf.com

The excellent sound system and convivial atmosphere make this one of San Francisco's best club-size music spots for quality rock, jazz or rhythm and blues acts most nights.
P7 ✉ 333 11th Street ☎ 415/255–0333 🚌 9, 12

SUNDANCE KABUKI CINEMA

www.sundancecinemas.com

This eight-screen modern movie complex is in Japantown.
L5 ✉ 1881 Post Street, at Fillmore Street ☎ 415/345–3243 🚌 2, 3, 38

THEATER RHINOCEROS

www.therhino.org

The diverse offerings at the home of the US's first gay and lesbian theater company often explore social attitudes and behavior. The theater was founded in 1977.
N8 ✉ 1360 Mission Street, Suite #200 ☎ 800/838–3006 🚌 14

TONGA ROOM

www.tongaroom.com

This Nob Hill bar is full of kitsch, rum drinks and even periodic tropical rainstorms.
P4 ✉ Fairmont Hotel, 950 Mason Street ☎ 415/772–5278 🕐 Wed, Thu, Sun 6–10pm, Fri–Sat 6–11pm 🚌 1; Powell–Hyde cable car

TORONADO

www.toronado.com

The various alternative lifestyles that are part and parcel of the Haight–Ashbury neighborhood can

be observed at this lively haunt.
📍 L7 ✉ 547 Haight Street ☎ 415/863–2276 🕐 Daily 11.30am–2am 🚌 6, 66, 71

TOSCA CAFÉ
www.toscacafesf.com
Opened in 1919 and allegedly serving the first espresso in California, Tosca has opera reverberating from its jukebox and numerous celebrity regulars including Nicolas Cage and Francis Ford Coppola.
📍 Q3 ✉ 242 Columbus Avenue ☎ 415/986–9651 🕐 Tue, Sun 5pm–midnight, Wed–Sat 5pm–2am 🚌 41

Chinatown at night

GUIDED CLUBBING

If deciding where to strut your stuff in the San Franciscan night proves impossible, you might relish the assistance of Three Babes and a Bus (☎ 800/414–0158), a company that will carry you—and a busload of similarly indecisive individuals—on a four-hour tour of some of the city's hottest nightspots (Saturday only). The $39 price includes admission and special ID, which allows you to walk straight in, even when there is a line of people.

WAR MEMORIAL OPERA HOUSE
www.sfwmpac.org/operahouse/oh_index.html
From September to December, this is the venue for the San Francisco Opera season. From February to May, the San Francisco Ballet appears here and it returns at Christmas for the Nutcracker.
📍 N6 ✉ 301 Van Ness Avenue ☎ 415/621–6600 🚇 Van Ness or Civic Center 🚌 5, 21, 47, 49, 80

YERBA BUENA CENTER FOR THE ARTS
www.ybca.org
This state-of-the art venue (▷ 63), with a 775-seat theater, has a strong program of contemporary music, dance and drama.
📍 Q5 ✉ 701 Mission Street ☎ 415/978–2787 🚇 Powell Street 🚌 14, 30, 45

YOSHI'S
www.yoshis.com
This much loved jazz club hosts live music and a top-class Japanese restaurant.
📍 L5 ✉ 1330 Fillmore Street ☎ 415/655–5600 🕐 Tue–Wed 5.30–9pm, Thu, Fri, Sat 5.30–10, Sun 5.30–9 🚌 22, 31

ENTERTAINMENT

PLAT DU JOUR

• SPECIALS •

Soups

- FRENCH ONION
- VEGETABLE w/ OREO

Special

BLT with goat cheese
on our homemade,
organic ciabatta

Come in for a glass
of beer or wine and
a salad or sandwich!

Eat

There are places to eat across the city to suit all tastes and budgets. In this section establishments are listed alphabetically.

Introduction

If Los Angeles has the lock on celebrities, then San Francisco has the lock on celebrity chefs—and first-rate chefs of the non-celebrity variety as well. When leading food magazines like *Bon Appetit* and *Gourmet* rank America's dining cities, San Francisco always rises to the top of the list, and for very good reason.

Culinary Melting Pot

With thousands of restaurants to choose from, it's difficult to think of a cuisine that can't be found here: dim sum that can compete with any you would find in Hong Kong; inexpensive, delicious and filling burritos, particularly good in the Mission District; increasingly good options for Indian and Pakistani food; unbelievably fresh sushi; enticing French bakeries; California cuisine in its many incarnations; plus great food influenced by Latin America, Asia and Europe.

Alice Waters

Of course, the culinary wonders aren't limited to San Francisco. Across the Bay is Berkeley's doyenne of food, Alice Waters. Her restaurant, Chez Panisse (▷ 112), is 40 years old, but her famously simple fare isn't showing signs of age. She "pioneered" a concept that has actually been around since the beginning of time: using seasonal, organic, local ingredients. She has influenced chefs domestically and abroad with her unpretentious menus that allow the fresh ingredients to assume the starring role.

EAT LIKE A SAN FRANCISCAN

Along with sustainable agriculture and socially responsible eating, the other trend that shows no sign of slowing down is the "small plates" craze. While some bemoan the practice, others embrace it as an opportunity to try extra dishes on the menu. Chefs are typically more inventive with appetizers and small plates, so be adventurous and sample a few.

From top: A tempting steak; a café in Haight-Ashbury; preparing shellfish at a restaurant in the Fisherman's Wharf area; a restaurant kitchen on Market Street

EAT

Directory

The Presidio

American
Liverpool Lil's
Presidio Social Club
Asian
Kabuto
Khan Toke
Ton Kiang
French
Baker Street Bistro
Italian
A16
Spruce
Mexican/Latin American
Mamacita

Pacific Heights to Telegraph Hill

American
Barney's Gourmet Hamburgers
Gary Danko
Izzy's Steaks & Chops
Asian
Alioto's
Betelnut
French
Café des Amis
Italian
Mario's Bohemian Cigar Store
North Beach Pizza
Rose Pistola
Mexican
Tacolicious
Spanish
Zarzuela
Vegetarian
Greens

Downtown to Nob Hill

American
Americano
Bix
Boulevard
Dottie's True Blue Café
Town Hall
Wayfare Tavern

Asian
Le Colonial
Gintane
House of Nanking
Lucky Creation
Shalimar
Slanted Door
French
Café Claude
Fleur de Lys
Fringale
Plouf
Greek
Kokkari Estiatorio
Italian
Perbacco

Western Addition to the Mission

American
Little Star Pizza
Max's
Monk's Kettle
Nopa
Asian
Dosa
Mifune
Tsunami Sushi Panhandle
Italian
Beretta
Delfina
Flour + Water
Mexican/Latin American
Las Tinajas
Taqueria Cancun

Golden Gate Park

Asian
Indian Oven
Thep Phanom

Farther Afield

Asian
Eric's Restaurant

Eating A–Z

<table>
<tr><td colspan="2">PRICES</td></tr>
</table>

Prices are approximate, based on a 3-course meal for one person.

$$$$	over $50
$$$	$31–$50
$$	$15–$30
$	under $15

A16 $$$

www.a16sf.com

You'll find wood-fired pizzas, dishes from Italy's Campania region and a wine list focusing on Southern Italian and California wines here.

✚ K3 ✉ 2355 Chestnut Street ☎ 415/771–2216 🕐 Wed–Fri lunch and dinner, Sat–Tue dinner 🚍 24, 30

ALIOTO'S $$$

www.aliotos.com

Alioto's is known for its delicious Sicilian seafood recipes. Enjoy your meal with a beautiful view over the Wharf.

✚ N2 ✉ 8 Fisherman's Wharf 415/673–0183 🕐 Mon–Sun 11am–11pm 🚃 Jefferson St and Taylor St cable car

Pizza is a popular option

AMERICANO $$$

www.americanorestaurant.com

In the Hotel Vitale, this restaurant serves tasty California cuisine. The spacious outdoor patio becomes a singles magnet after work.

✚ R4 ✉ 8 Mission Street ☎ 415/278–3777 🕐 Breakfast and dinner daily; Mon–Fri lunch 🚍 1, 14, 49

BAKER STREET BISTRO $$–$$$

www.bakerstreetbistro.com

Patrons tolerate cramped quarters in return for fantastic bistro fare at stunningly good prices.

✚ K3 ✉ 2953 Baker Street ☎ 415/931–1475 🕐 Tue–Fri lunch and dinner, Sat–Sun brunch and dinner 🚍 41, 45, 76

BARNEY'S GOURMET HAMBURGERS $$

www.barneyshamburgers.com

This is the place to come to enjoy fantastic burgers, curly fries and shakes, plus healthier options like soups and salads. The outdoor patio is an added bonus. There's another branch in Noe Valley (4138 24th Street), plus four East Bay locations.

✚ L3 ✉ 3344 Steiner Street ☎ 415/563–0307 🕐 Daily lunch and dinner 🚍 24, 30

BERETTA $$

www.berettasf.com

This Italian restaurant in the Mission District focuses on delicious thin-crust pizzas and cocktails crafted with expertise. For groups smaller than six, call ahead to add your name to the waiting list.

✚ Off map ✉ 1199 Valencia Street ☎ 415/695–1199 🕐 Mon–Fri dinner, Sat–Sun brunch, lunch and dinner 🚃 24th Street–Mission 🚍 14, 49

BETELNUT $$$

www.betelnutrestaurant.com

Asian fusion cuisine and great cocktails are the draw at this consistent Pacific Heights spot.

➕ L3 ✉ 2030 Union Street ☎ 415/929–8855 🕐 Tue–Sun lunch and dinner 🚌 41, 45

BIX $$$$

www.bixrestaurant.com

Tucked away on a downtown alley, this atmospheric supper club is always packed.

➕ Q3 ✉ 56 Gold Street (between Jackson and Pacific streets) ☎ 415/433–6300 🕐 Daily dinner, lunch Fri 🚌 3, 41

BOULEVARD $$$$

www.boulevardrestaurant.com

Try to nab a seat in the back room of this Embarcadero restaurant where you can gaze at Bay Bridge as you dive into superb New American cuisine. Dishes may include Sonoma foie gras, roasted sea bass and filet mignon.

➕ R4 ✉ 1 Mission Street ☎ 415/543–6084 🕐 Mon–Fri lunch and dinner, Sat–Sun dinner 🚌 1, 14, 41

CAFÉ DES AMIS $$$

www.cafedesamissf.com

A French newcomer in Cow Hollow, this brasserie has sleek black wood and marble floors. Menu items run the gamut from steak frites to lamb's tongue salad.

There's also a lively bar scene.

➕ L3 ✉ 2000 Union Street ☎ 415/563–7700 🕐 Daily lunch and dinner 🚌 41, 45

CAFÉ CLAUDE $$$

www.cafeclaude.com

Quintessentially French dishes like salad nicoise and onion soup are served in the downtown French quarter of the city, by Gallic waiters with a bit of attitude.

➕ Q4 ✉ 7 Claude Lane (between Grant and Kearny streets) ☎ 415/392–3505 🕐 Mon–Sat 11.30am–10.30pm, Sun 3.30–10.30pm 🚌 2, 3, 45

LE COLONIAL $$$

www.lecolonialsf.com

The ambience here evokes French-colonial Vietnam and a veranda beckons for fine-weather dining. Sample a snack from the bar or sit down to fully experience the California reworkings of Vietnamese dishes.

➕ P5 ✉ 20 Cosmo Place ☎ 415/931–3600 🕐 Mon–Fri dinner, Sat–Sun brunch, dinner 🚌 1, 2, 3, 27, 31, 76

DELFINA $$$

www.delfinasf.com

This Mission District trattoria serves its customers simple, delicious dishes that are made from top-notch ingredients.

➕ M9 ✉ 3621 18th Street ☎ 415/552–4055 🕐 Daily dinner 🚇 16th Street–Mission 🚌 14, 33

EAT

SOURDOUGH BREAD

The slightly bitter and chewy sourdough bread served in many San Franciscan restaurants first appeared here during the Gold Rush (and was first baked commercially by a French San Franciscan settler named Isadore Boudin). Yeast and baking powder were scarce and settlers made bread using a sour starter, a fermented mixture of flour and water that enabled the dough to rise. San Franciscan folklore holds that the quality of a sourdough loaf is dependent upon environmental conditions—in particular, the local fog.

DOSA $$$

www.dosasf.com

Enjoy South Indian fare in elegant surroundings in the Fillmore District. The original, smaller restaurant is in the Mission District (995 Valencia Street).

➕ L5 ✉ 1700 Fillmore Street
☎ 415/441–3672 🕐 Mon–Tue dinner, Wed–Sun lunch and dinner
🚌 22, 38

DOTTIE'S TRUE BLUE CAFÉ $$

This small, friendly diner close to Union Square serves up great start-the-day omelets. Later in the day, you can choose from a variety of healthy lunches.

➕ P5 ✉ 522 Jones Street ☎ 415/885–2767 🕐 Wed–Mon breakfast and lunch
🚌 27

ERIC'S RESTAURANT $$

Delicious Hunan and Mandarin cuisine is served in a clean white dining room overflowing with Noe Valley locals.

➕ Off map M9 ✉ 1500 Church Street
☎ 415/282–0919 🕐 Daily lunch and dinner 🚌 24, J

FLEUR DE LYS $$$$

www.hubertkeller.com/restaurants/fleur-de-lys.html

Fleur de Lys is more formal than many restaurants—jacket and tie are required—and serves San Francisco's best French food.

➕ P5 ✉ 777 Sutter Street ☎ 415/673–7779 🕐 Tue–Sat dinner 🚌 2, 3

FLOUR + WATER $$$

www.flourandwater.com

The small menu of seasonal Italian fare at this lauded restaurant typically includes home-made pastas, Neapolitan-style pizzas and cured meats.

➕ P9 ✉ 2401 Harrison Street ☎ 415/826–7000 🕐 Daily dinner 🚌 12, 27

FRINGALE $$$

www.fringalesf.com

Basque-French cuisine is dished up in an intimate but casual bistro close to the Metreon. The dessert menu is extensive and irresistible.

➕ R6 ✉ 570 4th Street ☎ 415/543–0573 🕐 Tue–Fri lunch and dinner, Sat–Mon dinner 🚇 Powell Street or Montgomery Street 🚌 9, 30, 45

GARY DANKO $$$$

www.garydanko.com

This is one of the city's finest restaurants, located in Russian Hill; choose from the three- to five-course tasting menu.

➕ N2 ✉ 800 North Point Street
☎ 415/749–2060 🕐 Daily dinner 🚌 19, 30; Powell–Hyde cable car

GINTANE $$

www.gitanerestaurant.com

This restaurant with three distinct dining areas manages to be both romantic and fun. Expect a modern southern Spanish menu showcasing seasonal produce.

➕ P5 ✉ 6 Claude Lane ☎ 415/788–6686 🕐 Mon–Tue 5.30–12pm, Wed–Fri 5.30pm–1am, Sat 5.30–12pm 🚌 1, 2, 3, 30, 41

GREENS $$$

www.greensrestaurant.com

Greens offers gourmet-pleasing vegetarian dishes using the produce of an organic farm run at

For a taste of Japan, try sushi

a Zen Buddhist retreat on the north side of San Francisco Bay. The bay views are as stunning as the food. Reserve ahead.

🔢 M2 ✉ Building A, Fort Mason Center ☎ 415/771–6222 🕐 Tue–Sat lunch and dinner, Sun brunch and dinner 🚌 22, 28, 30, 47, 49

HOUSE OF NANKING $

This tiny, popular eatery in Chinatown was among the first to bring Shanghai and northern Chinese cooking to San Francisco.

🔢 Q3 ✉ 919 Kearny Street ☎ 415/421–1429 🕐 Daily lunch and dinner 🚌 30, 41

INDIAN OVEN $$

www.indianovensf.com

This Haight spot whips up some of the best tandoori, naan and curry dishes in town.

🔢 L7 ✉ 233 Fillmore Street ☎ 415/626–1628 🕐 Daily lunch and dinner 🚌 6, 22, 66, 71

IZZY'S STEAKS & CHOPS $$$

www.izzyssteaks.com

A carnivore's paradise in the heart of the Marina, Izzy's Steaks &

Chops focuses on tender steak in all cuts.

🔢 L3 ✉ 3345 Steiner Street ☎ 415/563–0487 🕐 Mon–Sat dinner, Sun brunch and dinner 🚌 22, 76

KABUTO $$$

www.kabutosushi.com

A no-frills atmosphere at this Richmond District sushi bar keeps the focus on fresh raw fish.

🔢 F6 ✉ 5121 Geary Boulevard ☎ 415/752–5652 🕐 Tue–Sat lunch and dinner, Sun dinner 🚌 2, 29, 38

EAT

DIM SUM

Popular at lunchtime and for weekend brunch, dim sum consists of various small dishes offered to diners from carts. The cost is determined by the number of empty dishes on your table. Favorite dim sum dishes include *cha sil bow*—steamed pork bun; *chern goon*—spring rolls; *gai bow*—steamed chicken bun; and *sil mi*—steamed pork and shrimp dumplings. Rather less popular among Westerners are *gai guerk*—braised chicken feet; and *op guerk*—braised duck's feet.

KHAN TOKE $$

Be prepared to remove your shoes before dining on top-notch Thai cuisine at sunken tables.

➕ E6 ✉ 5937 Geary Boulevard
☎ 415/668–6654 🕐 Daily dinner
🚌 2, 29, 38

KOKKARI ESTIATORIO $$$

www.kokkari.com

This Financial District taverna serves a range of classic Greek favorites including *spanakopita* (spinach pie), moussaka and lamb dishes.

➕ R3 ✉ 200 Jackson Street ☎ 415/981–0983 🕐 Mon–Fri lunch and dinner, Sat–Sun dinner 🚇 Embarcadero 🚌 3, 12

LITTLE STAR PIZZA $$

www.littlestarpizza.com

Listen to the jukebox while you wait for tantalizing Chicago-style pizza in the Western Addition. (You'll find another branch in the Mission District.)

➕ K6 ✉ 846 Divisadero Street ☎ 415/441–1118 🕐 Tue–Sun dinner 🚌 24

LIVERPOOL LIL'S $$$

www.liverpoollils.com

It's a crime not to get a beer with your meal at this Pacific Heights saloon-cum-burger joint. You can dine on the sidewalk when weather permits.

➕ J3 ✉ 2942 Lyon Street
☎ 415/921–6664 🕐 Mon–Fri lunch and dinner, Sat–Sun brunch, lunch and dinner
🚌 30, 41, 45

LUCKY CREATION $

This tiny Chinatown hideaway serves adventurous vegetarian, and even a few vegan, versions of traditional Chinese food, including dim sum.

➕ Q4 ✉ 854 Washington Street
☎ 415/989–0818 🕐 Thu–Tue lunch and dinner 🚌 30, 45

MAMACITA $$

www.mamacitasf.com

The upscale authentic Mexican fare at this cantina comes with a lively singles scene at the bar and quite a bit of noise.

➕ K3 ✉ 2317 Chestnut Street
☎ 415/346–8494 🕐 Daily dinner
🚌 24, 30

MARIO'S BOHEMIAN CIGAR STORE $

This long-established North Beach café offers some excellent focaccia bread snacks.

➕ P3 ✉ 566 Columbus Avenue
☎ 415/362–0536 🕐 Daily lunch and dinner 🚌 30, 41, 45

MAX'S $–$$

www.maxsworld.com

While the New York-style deli fare is affordable and filling at this Bay Area chain, the real attraction is the opera-singing staff.

➕ N6 ✉ 601 Van Ness Avenue
☎ 415/771–7301 🕐 Mon–Fri lunch and dinner, Sat–Sun brunch, lunch and dinner
🚌 5, 47, 49

VEGETARIANS

If you don't eat meat, you still have plenty of dining options in the City by the Bay. In addition to Greens (▷ 144), noteworthy vegetarian establishments include Ananda Fuara (✉ 1298 Market Street ☎ 415/621–1994), in the Civic Center, and Millennium (✉ 580 Geary Street ☎ 415/345–3900), which serves imaginative organic and dairy-free entrées. Most Chinese and Indian restaurants also offer numerous vegetarian dishes.

Bread and cheese make a tasty snack…

…or try some seafood

MIFUNE $

www.mifune.com

Fast-food Japanese-style is served to fast-moving customers here; the noodle dishes are excellent.

🔲 L5 ✉ Japan Center, 1737 Post Street, Japantown ☎ 415/922–0337 🕐 Daily lunch and dinner 🚌 38

MONK'S KETTLE $$

www.monkskettle.com

This Mission District gastropub serves small and large plates meant to pair nicely with the dozens of beers on the menu. It stays open until late.

🔲 M8 ✉ 3141 16th Street ☎ 415/865–9523 🕐 Daily lunch and dinner 🚇 16th Street–Mission 🚌 22, 26

NOPA $$$

www.nopasf.com

Short for "north of the Panhandle", this former bank in the Western Addition now serves organic California fare past midnight in a lively, loud atmosphere.

🔲 K7 ✉ 560 Divisadero Street ☎ 415/864–8643 🕐 Mon–Fri dinner, Sat–Sun brunch and dinner 🚌 24

NORTH BEACH PIZZA $

www.northbeachpizza.com

The thick, chewy pizzas with a host of toppings, famous throughout the city, often result in a line outside in the evening.

🔲 Q3 ✉ 1462 Grant Avenue ☎ 415/433–2444 🕐 Daily lunch and dinner 🚌 30, 41, 45

PERBACCO $$$

www.perbaccosf.com

This downtown Italian gets high marks for its Piedmont and Ligurian cuisine.

🔲 R4 ✉ 230 California Street ☎ 415/955–0663 🕐 Mon–Fri lunch and dinner, Sat dinner 🚌 1, 41; California Street cable car

PLOUF $$–$$$

www.ploufsf.com

You can eat outdoors in good weather at this downtown bistro on a pedestrian-only alley. Tasty seafood is the focus; mussels are the house specialty.

🔲 Q4 ✉ 40 Belden Place ☎ 415/986–6491 🕐 Mon–Fri lunch and dinner, Sat dinner 🚌 1, 3, 30, 45, 76

EAT

PRESIDIO SOCIAL CLUB $$$

www.presidiosocialclub.com
Once an old army barracks, this
Presidio restaurant now serves
classic cocktails and American
comfort food, like roast chicken
and macaroni and cheese.
➕ J3 ✉ 563 Ruger Street ☎ 415/885–
1888 ⓘ Daily lunch and dinner; also
brunch Sat–Sun 🚌 28, 29, 41, 43, 45

ROSE PISTOLA $$$

www.rosepistolasf.com
This North Beach haunt has an
open kitchen, wood-burning oven
and a menu inspired by Italy's
Liguria region. There's live jazz
Thursday to Sunday.
➕ P3 ✉ 532 Columbus Avenue
☎ 415/399–0499 ⓘ Daily lunch and
dinner 🚌 30, 41, 45

SHALIMAR $

www.shalimarsf.com
Great naan is the tip of the iceberg
at this budget Indian-Pakistani spot
in the Tenderloin area. Cash only.
There's a second branch on Polk.
➕ P5 ✉ 532 Jones Street ☎ 415/928–
0333 ⓘ Daily lunch and dinner 🚌 38

SLANTED DOOR $$$

www.slanteddoor.com
Slanted Door serves modern
Vietnamese cuisine in a spacious
setting overlooking the Bay. For
quicker, cheaper fare, visit Out the
Door, the restaurant's to-go counter in the Ferry Building's main hall.
➕ R4 ✉ 1 Ferry Building ☎ 415/861–
8032 ⓘ Daily lunch, afternoon tea and
dinner 🚌 2, 6, 9, 14, 21, 31

SPRUCE $$$$

www.sprucesf.com
This Laurel Heights restaurant
serves a Mediterranean- and
Italian-influenced menu in
sophisticated, inviting surroundings.
➕ J5 ✉ 3640 Sacramento Street
☎ 415/931–5100 ⓘ Mon–Fri lunch and
dinner, Sat–Sun dinner 🚌 1, 3, 43

TACOLICIOUS $–$$

www.tacolicioussf.com
Fresh, flavorful tacos and ceviche
offset the cramped, loud quarters
at this new Marina favorite.
➕ L3 ✉ 2031 Chestnut Street
☎ 415/346–1966 ⓘ Daily lunch and
dinner 🚌 22, 30

Mexican tortilla chips and a bean dip

A plate of dim sum

TAQUERIA CANCUN $

Burritos in many different varieties and other well-prepared Mexican favorites are the staples in this busy eatery in the Mission District. Another branch is located at 3211 Mission Street.

➕ N9 ✉ 2288 Mission Street ☎ 415/252-9560 🕐 Daily breakfast, lunch and dinner 🚌 14, 49

THEP PHANOM $$

www.thepphanom.com

Hot and spicy Thai cuisine is served here, in the Lower Heights neighborhood.

➕ L7 ✉ 400 Waller Street ☎ 415/431-2526 🕐 Daily dinner 🚌 6, 22, 66, 71

LAS TINAJAS $$

This relaxed restaurant serves some of the best Nicaraguan food in the whole of the city. The platters come highly recommended.

➕ N9 ✉ 2338 Mission Street ☎ 415/695-9933 🕐 Mon–Sat 10am–4.30pm 🚇 16th Street–Mission 🚌 14, 49

TON KIANG $$

www.tonkiang.net

Spread over two Richmond District floors and frequented mainly for its excellent Hong-Kong style dim sum, Ton Kiang also offers a Hakka-style dinner menu.

➕ E6 ✉ 5821 Geary Boulevard ☎ 415/387-8273 🕐 Daily lunch and dinner 🚌 2, 29, 38

TOWN HALL $$$

www.townhallsf.com

This former warehouse turned SoMa restaurant focuses on regional American fare with exciting New Orleans influences. Menus have included buttermilk

---

CARNIVOROUS CRAVINGS

Meat lovers have many options in the city. Harris' (✉ 2100 Van Ness ☎ 415/673–1888) serves steaks and ribs to perfection in Russian Hill. Nearby is House of Prime Rib (✉ 1906 Van Ness ☎ 415/885–4605). Cow Hollow's Brazen Head (✉ 3166 Buchanan Street ☎ 415/921–7600) is known for its peppercorn steak.

---

fried chicken and cornmeal fried oysters.

➕ R5 ✉ 342 Howard Street ☎ 415/908-3900 🕐 Mon–Sat lunch and dinner, Sun dinner 🚌 6, 10, N–Judah

TSUNAMI SUSHI PANHANDLE $$$

www.dajanigroup.net/establishments/tsunami-sushi-panhandle

Dine on unusual rolls at low tables at this hip Western Addition sushi spot, with countless sake options on offer too.

➕ K6 ✉ 1306 Fulton Street ☎ 415/567-7664 🕐 Mon–Sat dinner 🚌 24

WAYFARE TAVERN $$$

www.wayfaretavern.com

Celebrity chef Tyler Florence's three-story Financial District restaurant serves American fare in a men's club-style atmosphere.

➕ Q4 ✉ 558 Sacramento Street ☎ 415/772-9060 🕐 Mon–Sat lunch and dinner, Sun dinner 🚌 1, 3, 8X, 10, 12, 30, 41; California Street cable car

ZARZUELA $$–$$$

If you can brave the dire parking situation in Russian Hill, the Spanish tapas, paella and sangria here are worth the effort.

➕ N3 ✉ 2000 Hyde Street ☎ 415/346-0800 🕐 Tue–Sat dinner 🚌 41, 45; Powell–Hyde cable car

EAT

Sleep

Ranging from luxurious and modern upmarket hotels to simple budget hostels, San Francisco has accommodations to suit everyone. In this section establishments are listed alphabetically.

SLEEP

Introduction

San Francisco has a huge range of accommodations. The city is compact and fairly
easy to navigate by public transportation
or by car, so location here is less important
than it is in larger cities. Booking ahead
is crucial, however, especially during the
high season.

Hotels
Full-service hotels are primarily in the downtown, SoMa and Nob Hill neighborhoods of
San Francisco. You'll pay more, of course, for
the location and the amenities, which will likely
include a fitness room or gym, laundry service,
in-room internet access and safes, valet parking
and concierge. Swimming pools are not as
prevalent in San Francisco as they are in Los
Angeles, but several hotels do have them. Most
hotels do not include breakfast or parking in
their rates, but many allow children to share a
room with their parents free of charge.

Motels
Many motels belong to chains and offer reliabil-
ity and good value; they're ideal for a brief
stopover. The majority of San Francisco's motels
are along Lombard Street in the Marina District,
in the northern section of the city. The street is
a busy thoroughfare to the Golden Gate Bridge
and Highway 101, but it's also near shops,
restaurants and some notable attractions.
Motels typically offer cable TV and hair dryers.

OTHER OPTIONS

There are a number of hostels in San Francisco that
charge as little as $25–$30 per night per person. Most
have single-sex dorms, although some may also have
family rooms. Contact American Youth Hostels (www.
hiusa.org). B&Bs can be a more personal alternative to a
hotel, but keep in mind that they often require two-night
minimum stays on weekends and three-night minimum
stays during holidays.

*San Francisco has a large choice of accommodations,
but be sure to book ahead*

SLEEP

Directory

The Presidio

Mid-Range
Laurel Inn

Pacific Heights to Telegraph Hill

Budget
Hostelling International San
    Francisco Fisherman's Wharf
San Remo Hotel
Town House Motel

Mid-Range
Hotel Boheme
Hotel Majestic
Hotel del Sol
Marina Motel
Tuscan

Luxury
Argonaut Hotel
Hotel Drisco
Washington Square Inn

Downtown to Nob Hill

Budget
Adelaide Hotel & Hostel
Hostelling International San
    Francisco City Center
Hostelling International San
    Francisco Downtown
Hotel des Arts
Hotel Metropolis
Hotel Stratford

Mid-Range
Hotel Bijou
Hotel Diva
Hotel Griffon
Hotel Rex
Renoir Hotel

Luxury
Campton Place
Clift
Fairmont San Francisco
Four Seasons
Mandarin Oriental
The Palace Hotel
Ritz-Carlton San Francisco
Westin St. Francis
White Swan Inn
W Hotel

Western Addition to the Mission

Mid-Range
Chateau Tivoli
Hotel Tomo
Inn at the Opera
Phoenix Hotel
Sleep Over Sauce

Golden Gate Park

Mid-Range
Red Victorian Bed, Breakfast & Art
Stanyan Park Hotel

Luxury
Cavallo Point

Farther Afield

Budget
24 Henry
Willows Inn

SLEEP

Sleeping A–Z

PRICES

Prices are approximate and based on a double room for one night.

$$$	over $200
$$	$120–$200
$	under $120

24 HENRY $
www.24henry.com
A five-room guest house in the Castro district, 24 Henry is gay and lesbian friendly. Breakfast is included.
➕ L9 ✉ 24 Henry Street ☎ 415/864–5686 🚌 24, 37

ADELAIDE HOTEL & HOSTEL $
www.adelaidehostel.com
This Financial District pension offers dorms, private rooms and rooms for families (up to four people) at the original location and in two nearby buildings on Post.
➕ P5 ✉ 5 Isadora Duncan Court (off Taylor Street, between Geary and

BED-AND-BREAKFAST

San Francisco's bed-and-breakfast inns offer a friendly alternative to hotels. Bed-and-breakfast owners often serve a healthy home-cooked breakfast, and will readily pass on their knowledge of the city. Reflecting the fact that both the individual properties and the rooms within them can vary greatly, bed-and-breakfast establishments span all price categories and are found all over the city. Advance reservation is always recommended. Bed-and-breakfast accommodations can be arranged through Bed & Breakfast San Francisco; for reservations go online at www.bbsf.com or telephone ☎ 800/452–8249.

Post streets) ☎ 877/359–1915
🚌 2, 3, 38, 76

ARGONAUT HOTEL $$$
www.argonauthotel.com
The nautical theme at this Fisherman's Wharf hotel is fitting for its location. Rooms are airy, WiFi is complimentary. It's pet-friendly and has 265 rooms.
➕ N2 ✉ 495 Jefferson Street ☎ 415/563–0800
🚌 19, 30, 47, 91, F; Powell-Hyde cable car

CAMPTON PLACE $$$
www.tajhotels.com/camptonplace
Well placed close to Union Square, Campton Place has 110 stylish rooms and attentive staff.
➕ Q5 ✉ 340 Stockton Street ☎ 415/781–5555 🚌 30, 45

CAVALLO POINT $$
www.cavallopoint.com
This spectacular hotel in the national park has rooms with sweeping views of the Golden Gate Bridge and Bay Area. There are both historic and contemporary rooms, an excellent restaurant and state-of-the-art spa.
➕ J7 ✉ 601 Murray Circle Fort Baker ☎ 888/651–2003 or 415/339–4700
🚌 Free hotel shuttle bus from ferry at Sausalito

CHATEAU TIVOLI $$
www.chateautivoli.com
An amiable and historic Victorian B&B near Alamo Square, Chateau Tivoli has nine rooms and suites. It serves a generous weekend brunch, as well as afternoon cheese and wine.
➕ L6 ✉ 1057 Steiner Street ☎ 415/776–5462 or 800/228–1647 🚌 5, 21

CLIFT $$$

www.clifthotel.com

This Philippe Starck-designed hotel has a whimsical lobby, 378 guest rooms, and the famed art deco-style Redwood Room bar.

✚ P5 ✉ 495 Geary Street ☎ 415/775–4700 or 800/697–1791 🚌 38

FAIRMONT SAN FRANCISCO $$$

www.fairmont.com/sanfrancisco

This famous Nob Hill landmark hotel has 591 sumptuous rooms and suites affording lovely views.

✚ P4 ✉ 950 Mason Street ☎ 866/540–4491 or 415/772–5000 🚌 1; Powell–Hyde cable car

FOUR SEASONS $$$

www.fourseasons.com/sanfrancisco

This elegant hotel has 277 spacious rooms and suites. Guests can use the Sports Club/LA gym.

✚ Q5 ✉ 757 Market Street ☎ 415/633–3000 🚌 Any Market Street bus

HOSTELLING INTERNATIONAL SAN FRANCISCO $

www.sfhostels.com

More than 600 hostel beds, mostly in small dorms with some private rooms, are available at the three sites of Hostelling International: City Center, Downtown and Fisherman's Wharf (Fort Mason). All three offer luggage storage, self-catering kitchens and internet access, and all can be easily reached by bus.

City Center ✚ N5 ✉ 685 Ellis Street ☎ 415/474–5721 🚌 27

Downtown ✚ P5 ✉ 312 Mason Street ☎ 415/788–5604 🚌 38

Fisherman's Wharf ✚ M2 ✉ Building 240, Fort Mason ☎ 415/771–7277 🚌 28, 49

TELEPHONING HOTELS

Many hotels and some bed-and-breakfast inns can be telephoned using toll-free numbers (prefixed 800, 888, 877 or 866). Remember that these numbers can usually be dialed from anywhere in the United States or Canada, although there is sometimes a different toll-free number for calls made within California (and a few numbers may be available in California only).

HOTEL DES ARTS $–$$

www.sfhoteldesarts.com

As the name suggests, local artists have decorated this hotel, and their work also features in the gallery. The least costly of the 43 rooms have washbasins and shared bathrooms, while others have private facilities. A continental breakfast is served.

✚ Q4 ✉ 447 Bush Street ☎ 800/956–4322 or 415/956–3232 🚌 2, 3, 76

HOTEL BIJOU $$

www.hotelbijou.com

San Francisco-set movies provide the cue for the 65 themed rooms here, close to Union Square. Breakfast is included.

✚ P5 ✉ 111 Mason Street ☎ 800/771–1022 or 415/771–1200 🚌 38

HOTEL BOHEME $$

www.hotelboheme.com

Evoking 1950s North Beach, this cozy hotel with 15 small rooms plays up its connection to the literary Beat movement.

✚ P3 ✉ 444 Columbus Avenue ☎ 415/433–9111 🚌 30, 41, 45

HOTEL DIVA $$

www.hoteldiva.com

SLEEP

Reservations should be made as early as possible. A deposit (usually by credit card) equivalent to the nightly rate should ensure your room is held at least until 6pm; if you are arriving later, inform the hotel. Credit card is the usual payment method; traveler's checks or cash can be used but payment will then be expected in advance. The total charge will include the city's 14 percent accommodations tax.

Smack in the middle of the theater district, the Diva has 116 rooms with lots of chrome and other modern touches, though it can feel a bit sanitized.

P5 440 Geary Street 415/885–0200 or 800/553–1900 38

HOTEL DRISCO $$$

www.hoteldrisco.com
Breakfast and evening wine are included in the cost of this 48-room hotel, built in 1903, in well-heeled Pacific Heights.

K4 2901 Pacific Avenue
800/634–7277 or 415/346–2880
3, 24

A bay-view room, Mandarin Oriental

HOTEL GRIFFON $$–$$$

www.hotelgriffon.com
This Embarcadero boutique hotel has 57 rooms and five suites, many with Bay Bridge views. Continental breakfast is included in the room price.

R4 155 Steuart Street 415/495–2100 or 800/321–2201 1, 14, 41

HOTEL MAJESTIC $$

www.thehotelmajestic.com
Formerly a private residence, this attractive hotel has 52 European-style rooms in Lower Pacific Heights. Many rooms have claw-foot bathtubs and are decked out with antique furnishings.

M5 1500 Sutter Street 415/441–1100 or 800/869–8966 47, 49

HOTEL METROPOLIS $

www.hotelmetropolis.com
While its Tenderloin location is not to everyone's taste, this 105-room hotel, decorated with bright colors, is about five blocks from Union Square and is also close to the theater district.

P5 25 Mason Street 415/775–4600 or 800/736–3766 Any Market Street bus; Powell–Hyde cable car

HOTEL REX $$

www.jdvhotels.com/rex
The lobby of this welcoming downtown hotel is filled with old books and the 94 rooms have a French country theme. There is live jazz on Friday nights in the lobby.

P5 562 Sutter Street 415/433–4434 or 800/433–4434 2, 3, 76

HOTEL DEL SOL $$

www.jdvhotels.com/del_sol
Bold, playful colors decorate this converted motor lodge in the

Marina. The 57 rooms surround
a pool.

➕ L5 ✉ 3100 Webster Street ☎ 415/
921–5520 or 877/433–5765 🚌 22, 30

HOTEL STRATFORD $

www.hotelstratford.com

Very reasonably priced, quality
budget hotel that is centrally
located just off Union Square. The
free bottled water and friendly staff
are a definite plus.

➕ Q5 ✉ 242 Powell Street ☎ 888/688–
0038 🚌 30, 45

HOTEL TOMO $$

www.jdvhotels.com/tomo

This Japantown hotel has Japanese
pop art, a wall of TVs playing movies in the lobby, and gaming suites,
plus 125 rooms.

➕ L5 ✉ 1800 Sutter Street ☎ 415/921–
4000 or 800/738–7477 🚌 2, 3, 76

INN AT THE OPERA $$–$$$

www.shellhospitality.com/hotels/
inn-at-the-opera

Quiet and elegant Inn at the Opera
is a favorite of thespians and
opera stars for its proximity to the
performing-arts halls of Civic
Center. There are 48 rooms.

➕ M6 ✉ 333 Fulton Street ☎ 800/325–
2708 or 415/863–8400 🚌 5, 21

LAUREL INN $$

www.jdvhotels.com/laurel_inn

In a quiet part of town, this Laurel
Heights lodge has 49 rooms,
some with kitchenettes. It's near
Sacramento Street shops.

➕ J5 ✉ 444 Presidio Avenue
☎ 415/567–8467 or 800/738–7977
🚌 1, 43

MANDARIN ORIENTAL $$$

www.mandarin-oriental.com/sanfrancisco

Mandarin Oriental is in the heart
of the Financial District with 158
large, opulently furnished rooms,
some of which have city views.

➕ Q4 ✉ 222 Sansome Street
☎ 800/622–0404 or 415/276–9888
🚌 31, 38, 41

MARINA MOTEL $$

www.marinamotel.com

This plain and simple 39-room
motel on the northern edge of
Pacific Heights offers guests a
choice of regular and kitchen-
equipped rooms.

➕ K3 ✉ 2576 Lombard Street ☎ 800/
346–6118 or 415/921–9406 🚌 28, 43, 76

THE PALACE HOTEL $$$

www.sfpalace.com

The city's first luxury hotel is
located downtown. It's appropriate
for royalty, heads of state and
anyone with a taste for the finer
things (553 rooms).

➕ Q5 ✉ 2 New Montgomery Street
☎ 800/325–3589 or 415/512–1111
🚇 Montgomery Street 🚌 5, 6, 9, 21, 31,
38, 45, 71

PETIT AUBERGE $$

www.petiteaubergesf.com

The Provencal floral decor and
complimentary wine and hors

SPA DAYS

Many fine hotels tempt guests with
luxurious spas, but the elite pampering
destination in San Francisco is on Nob Hill
at the 11,000sq ft (1,220sq m) Nob Hill
Spa (✉ 1075 California Street
☎ 415/345–2888), located inside the
Huntington Hotel. The decadence includes
facials, massages, Jacuzzi and saunas, an
indoor infinity pool, yoga, Pilates and
wellness workshops.

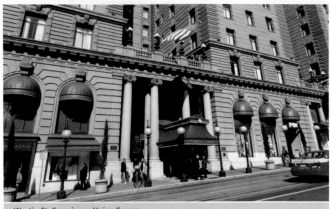
Westin St. Francis, on Union Square

d'oeuvres served fireside in the parlour combine to give this little hotel a homely feel. It's in a central location just off Union Square.

➕ P5 ✉ 863 Bush Street ☎ 800/365–3004 or 415/928–6000 🚌 38

PHOENIX HOTEL $$

www.jdvhotels.com/phoenix

This self-proclaimed rocker hotel is in the tough Tenderloin neighborhood and close to popular music venues. It has 44 rooms, along with a courtyard pool and a new bar and lounge.

➕ N5 ✉ 601 Eddy Street
☎ 415/776–1380 or 800/248–9466
🚌 19, 31, 47

RED VICTORIAN BED, BREAKFAST & ART $$

www.redvic.com

The 18 themed guest rooms here include the Flower Child Room, the Skylight Room and the Summer of Love Room. It's in historic Haight-Ashbury, near to Golden Gate Park.

➕ J7 ✉ 1655 Haight Street ✉ 415/864–1978 🚌 6, 43, 71, N–Judah

RENOIR HOTEL $$

www.renoirhotel.com

A likeable flatiron-shape Civic Center landmark, the Renoir Hotel houses 133 simple but comfortable rooms. Be aware that the Market Street side can be noisy.

➕ P6 ✉ 45 McAllister Street
☎ 415/626–5200 or 800/576–3388
🚌 Any Market Street bus

RITZ-CARLTON SAN FRANCISCO $$$

www.ritzcarlton.com/sanfrancisco

After a $12.5 million renovation, this branch of the luxury chain is more grand than ever, with amenities like 400-thread-count sheets and stellar customer service. There are 336 rooms.

➕ P4 ✉ 600 Stockton Street
☎ 415/296–7465 or 800/241–3333
🚌 1, 2, 3, 30, 45, 91; Powell-Hyde cable car, California Street cable car

SAN REMO HOTEL $

www.sanremohotel.com

On the outskirts of North Beach, this 1906 Victorian building has

62 small rooms, although none has a private bathroom.
➕ P2 ✉ 2237 Mason Street
☎ 415/776–8688 or 800/352–7366
🚌 9, 30

SLEEP OVER SAUCE $$
www.sleepsf.com
This 1906 Hayes Valley house is now an eight-room urban guest house. It sits above the restaurant Sauce, hence the name.
➕ M7 ✉ 135 Gough Street ☎ 415/621–0896 🚌 21, Market Street buses

STANYAN PARK HOTEL $$
www.stanyanpark.com
Stanyan Park is a 36-room friendly hotel next to Golden Gate Park. Breakfast is included.
➕ H8 ✉ 750 Stanyan Street
☎ 415/751–1000 🚌 6, 33, 43, 66, 71

TOWN HOUSE MOTEL $
www.sftownhousemotel.com
This 23-room motel is simply furnished, well kept and in a convenient Marina location. It serves a continental breakfast.
➕ M3 ✉ 1650 Lombard Street
☎ 800/255–1516 or 415/885–5163 🚌 76

THE TUSCAN $$
www.tuscaninn.com
There is an upmarket Italian restaurant at this Fisherman's Wharf hotel with 221 rooms on four floors. Pets are allowed.
➕ P2 ✉ 425 North Point Street
☎ 415/561–1100 or 800/648–4626
🚌 30

WASHINGTON SQUARE INN $$$
www.wsisf.com
This boutique hotel has prime real estate on this lovely North Beach

square. A few of the 15 rooms have views of Coit Tower.
➕ P3 ✉ 1660 Stockton Street
☎ 415/981–4220 or 800/388–0220
🚌 30, 41, 45

WESTIN ST. FRANCIS $$$
www.westinstfrancis.com
Westin St. Francis has been a San Franciscan landmark since 1904 and is resoundingly aristocratic. There are nearly 1,200 rooms.
➕ P5 ✉ 335 Powell Street at Union Square ☎ 800/WESTIN 1 or 415/397–7000
🚌 2, 3, 6, 38, 71; Powell–Hyde or Powell–Mason cable car

WHITE SWAN INN $$$
www.whiteswaninns.com
A breakfast buffet and complimentary evening wine add to the already rich atmosphere of this Nob Hill 26-room, antique-decorated inn.
➕ P4 ✉ 845 Bush Street ☎ 800/999–9570 or 415/775–1755 🚌 2, 3, 76

WILLOWS INN $
www.willowssf.com
This gay-friendly Castro inn has 12 rooms, each with a washbasin, and shared bathrooms down the hall. Continental breakfast is included.
➕ L8 ✉ 710 14th Street ☎ 415/431–4770 or 800/431–0277 🚌 Any Market Street bus

W HOTEL $$$
www.wsanfrancisco.com
A modern SoMa property close to the San Francisco Museum of Modern Art and downtown, this hotel has 404 rooms, a lap pool, Bliss Spa and the lively XYZ Bar.
➕ Q5 ✉ 181 3rd Street ☎ 415/777–5300 or 888/627–8391 🚌 14, 30, 45

MARKET STREET &
POWELL
AND
MARKET
11
HYDE - BEACH
FISHERMANS
WHARF
CAREFUL,
IT'S A TRAP.

FISHERMANS WHARF

Need to Know

This section takes you through all the practical aspects of your trip to make it run more smoothly and to give you confidence before you go and while you are there.

NEED TO KNOW

Planning Ahead

WHEN TO GO

San Francisco's peak tourist months are July and August and hotels are busy. September and October are better times to visit, as the crowds have thinned and the weather is warm and sunny. Take a sweater and jacket for evening as fogs off the Pacific Ocean can chill the air.

TIME

San Francisco is on Pacific Time, eight hours behind the UK and nine hours behind Western Europe.

TEMPERATURE

JAN	FEB	MAR	APR	MAY	JUN	JUL	AUG	SEP	OCT	NOV	DEC
55°F	54°F	55°F	55°F	61°F	61°F	61°F	61°F	70°F	70°F	61°F	54°F
13°C	12°C	13°C	13°C	16°C	16°C	16°C	16°C	21°C	21°C	16°C	12°C

Spring (March to May) fogs usually occur only in the morning and have lifted by midday as the temperature rises.

Summer (June to August) weather is unpredictable. One day may be warm and sunny and the next a chilly fog appears in the morning and lingers through the evening.

Fall (September to November) sees the warmest and clearest days of the year.

Winter (December to February) rain can be heavy, especially in January. There are often torrential storms and it can rain for several days. Most rainfall occurs during the winter months.

WHAT'S ON

January/February *Chinese New Year*: Two weeks of Chinatown festivities; date depends on lunar cycle.

March *St. Patrick's Day* (Mar 17): Irish and would-be-Irish dress in green for a parade on Market Street.

April *Cherry Blossom Festival*: Japantown celebrates Japanese art and culture.

May *Cinco de Mayo* (May 5): Mexican celebration centered in the Mission District.

Bay to Breakers: Athletes and exhibitionists race from one side of the city to the other.

Carnaval: The Mission District fills with music, floats and costumes.

June *Gay Pride Parade*: Huge march, usually starting or ending at Civic Center Plaza.

North Beach Festival: Music, food and sidewalk chalk art.

July *Independence Day* (Jul 4): Fireworks and a 50-cannon salute on the northern waterfront.

San Francisco Marathon: The country's third-largest marathon crosses Golden Gate Bridge.

August *Outside Lands Music and Arts Festival*: A multi-day festival in Golden Gate Park.

September *Shakespeare in the Park*: Free outdoor performances in the Presidio. Each summer features a different play by the Bard.

October *Fleet Week*: The US Navy's Blue Angels do a popular and daring air show, and they fly under the Golden Gate Bridge.

November *Day of the Dead* (Nov 2): Mexican tribute to the spirit world, with a parade through the Mission District.

December *Tchaikovsky's Nutcracker:* In a winter tradition, the San Francisco Ballet performs at the War Memorial Opera House.

SAN FRANCISCO ONLINE

San Francisco has excellent websites with regularly updated information on everything from the theater to news, weather and gossip.

www.citysearch.com/guide/sanfrancisco-ca-metro
Professional reviews with local tips covering shops, restaurants, nightspots, museums, cinemas, theaters and more.

www.sfstation.com
Cutting-edge nightclubs, bars and stores.

www.theatrebayarea.org
Theater news and listings.

www.nps.gov
Factual information on the city's federally run parks, including Alcatraz.

www.diggers.org
Tells the story of the proto-hippie Diggers, active in Haight–Ashbury in the mid-1960s and full of radical ideas even today.

www.sfgate.com
The *San Francisco Chronicle* website, with dining, nightlife and events news.

www.sfbg.com
www.sfweekly.com
The influential websites of the free papers *San Francisco Bay Guardian* and *SF Weekly*.

www.sanfran.com
San Francisco magazine dispenses ideas for elegant shopping, dining and generally spending money around town.

www.511.org
Brings Bay Area travel, be it by car, bike, bus, train or plane, into a single site.

www.flavorpill.com/sanfrancisco
A guide to events in the city, from quirky to mainstream.

PRIME TRAVEL SITES

www.bart.gov
www.sfmta.com
Timetables, routes and fares.
www.ci.sf.ca.us
The city's administration provides more practical information.
www.fodors.com
A travel-planning site where you can research prices and weather, book tickets, cars and rooms and ask fellow travelers questions; links to other sites.

INTERNET CAFÉS

Most hotels and many cafés and bars in San Francisco offer free or low-cost internet access, including the Starbucks and Coffee Bean & Tea Leaf chains. The following stand out in this fully wired city:

● Gallery Café (✉ 1200 Mason Street ☎ 415/296–9932) has organic breads, gourmet coffee and free internet access.
● Sugar Café (✉ 679 Sutter Street ☎ 415/ 441–5678) is open day and evening for food and alcohol.
● Quetzal (✉ 1234 Polk Street ☎ 415/673–4181) sells green coffees and a range of fruit smoothies.

Getting There

ENTRY REQUIREMENTS

Visitors from outside the US must show a passport valid for at least six months. You must have a return or onward ticket. Visitors from the UK who are eligible for the Visa Waiver Program, and eligible visitors from other countries with visa waiver status, must register with the US's Electronic System for Travel Authorization (ESTA™). Register online at https://esta.cbp.dhs.gov/esta at least 72 hours prior to travel, preferably much earlier. This is valid for stays of 90 days or less. For further details, or for visa information for longer stays, go online at www.usembassy.org.uk. Always check the latest entry requirements before traveling. Note that due to heightened security measures, it may take longer to pass through security checkpoints at the airport.

CULTURE AT SFO

In the International Terminal you'll find the San Francisco Airport Commission Aviation Library and Louis A. Turpen Aviation Museum, which chronicles the history of aviation through photographs and objects. In addition, the San Francisco Arts Commission selects the permanent art—including paintings, sculptures and mosaics—that is displayed throughout the airport.

AIRPORTS

There are direct flights to San Francisco from all over the world. The main airport is San Francisco International (SFO). You can also fly into Oakland International Airport and San Jose International.

San Francisco

Oakland International
17 miles (27km)

SFO
14 miles (23km)

San Jose Internatinal
45 miles (73km)

FROM SFO

San Francisco International Airport (tel 650/821–8211; www.flysfo.com) is 14 miles (23km) south of the city. BART (tel 415/989–2278) runs directly to the city from the airport, cost $8.10, and takes around 30 minutes. Airport Express Coaches (tel 415/775–5121) take visitors from the airport to the city every 30 minutes between 4.30am and 10pm, cost $17 one way, and take an hour to make the journey. Privately run minibuses such as SuperShuttle (tel 650/558–8500) pick up from the traffic island outside and cost approximately $17 per person. A taxi into the city costs around $60.

FROM OAKLAND INTERNATIONAL

Oakland International Airport (tel 510/563–3300; www.flyoakland.com), which serves both domestic and international flights, is across the Bay, 17 miles (27km) from San Francisco. You travel into the city via I-880 and I-80; traffic on the Bay Bridge may make travel time longer. A taxi will get you to the city in about 35–45 minutes, costing around $50 one way, depending on your destination. Otherwise take the Air-BART shuttle to the

Coliseum/Oakland station, cost $3, and catch the next BART to the city; cost is around $3.80.

FROM SAN JOSE INTERNATIONAL

The city's third airport (tel 408/277–4759; www.sjc.org), although about 45 miles (73km) south of downtown San Francisco, is well served by domestic carriers. Take the VTA Airport Flyer (route 10) to Santa Clara station and then CalTrain (tel 800/660–4287) to the city, which takes about 80 minutes and costs $8.50.

MORE AIRPORT INFORMATION

Airport websites have a plethora of useful information, including the list of airlines that serve the airport, ground transportation, driving directions, maps and security status. Oakland's site even provides real-time weather and traffic reports. For up-to-date security information and precautions from the US Transportation Security Administration, check out the agency's comprehensive web-site, www.tsa.gov, and click on "For Travelers."

TEMPORARY TRANSBAY TERMINAL

San Francisco's Transbay Terminal at First and Mission streets is undergoing a massive $4.2 billion transformation. The new Transbay Transit Center will be a 1 million sq ft (93,000sq m) hub and landmark, with a 5.4-acre (2.2ha) public park on its roof. Until the new terminal opens in the summer of 2017, the Transbay Temporary Terminal (tel 415/977–0531; www.temporaryterminal.org) is located at Howard and Main streets.

ARRIVING BY BUS

Greyhound buses (tel 800/229–9424) into the city terminate at the Transbay Temporary Terminal (▷ above).

ARRIVING BY TRAIN

Amtrak (tel 800/872–7245; www.amtrak.com) serves Emeryville east of the city, and provides free shuttle buses from there to various stops in San Francisco.

INSURANCE

Traveler's insurance is strongly recommended. Keep in mind that there are two different types: Trip insurance can minimize your losses in the event that you have to cancel or delay a trip, while medical travel insurance protects you if you incur medical expenses while traveling (▷ 169). Check your current policy and buy supplementary cover if necessary.

VISITORS WITH DISABILITIES

Aside from its steep hills, San Francisco is generally a good city for visitors using a wheelchair, with ramped public buildings and accessible buses, BART stations and taxis. Some hotels have roll-in showers, and some have Braille signage. For details, see *Access San Francisco*, a free annually updated booklet published by Access Northern California (www.accessnca.com), available from the Convention & Visitors Bureau. Also contact the Mayor's Office on Disability (✉ 401 Van Ness Avenue, Room 300, San Francisco, CA 94102 ☎ 415/554–6789; www.ci.sf.ca.us/sfmod).

Getting Around

DRIVING

● Unless posted higher, the limit is 25mph (40kph) in school zones, business and residential areas.

● Maximum speed on freeways is 65mph (105kph), 70mph (113kph) where specifically posted, except on downtown freeways, where it is 55mph (89kph), and on construction zones.

● A right turn on a red light after stopping is legal unless posted otherwise, as is a left on red at the intersection of two one-way streets.

● There is a toll for drivers coming south across the Golden Gate Bridge, and west across the Bay Bridge.

● If you belong to a motoring organization, check its links with the AAA California State Automobile Association, which offers free maps to members (✉ 160 Sutter Street ☎ 415/773-1900).

Much of San Francisco can be explored on foot but the city has an excellent system of buses and cable cars, as well as the underground BART system, which is chiefly used for crossing the bay to Berkeley and Oakland. MUNI buses and metro trains (tel 415/673–MUNI) serve the outer neighborhoods. Use taxis if you are in a rush, traveling late at night or want to pass quickly through edgy neighborhoods. A MUNI Passport (www.sfmta.com/cms/mfares/passports.htm), which is valid on MUNI buses, streetcars and cable cars for one, three or seven days costs $15, $23 or $29 respectively. Muni Passports can be bought at the Visitor Information Center (▷ 170).

BART

Fares range from $1.75 to $10.55 according to distance traveled. Tickets can be bought from machines at BART stations. Operating times are Mon–Fri 4am–midnight, Sat 6am–midnight, Sun 8am–midnight. All BART stations display maps of the BART system. For further information tel 415/989–2278.

BIKING

Despite the hilly terrain, biking is a popular way to get around in San Francisco and avoid the hassles of parking. Rentals are available all over the city, including Blazing Saddles (1095 Columbus Avenue and Pier 41, among other locations; tel 415/202–8888); and Bay City Bike (2661 Taylor Street, 501 Bay Street and 1325 Columbus Avenue; tel 415/346–2453).

BUSES

Buses cover the entire city, operating 5am–1am; outside these hours Owl Service buses provide a reduced-frequency service on main routes. The flat fare is currently $2; to change buses on a single ride, ask the driver for a free transfer ticket. Exact change is necessary and should be fed into the machine next to the driver when boarding. Bus routes are shown in the phone book and at most bus stops. Maps and timetables are available from City Hall and, in a style more accessible for

visitors (and including BART routes), from the
Visitor Center Hallidie Plaza.

CABLE CARS

Cable cars, more a tourist attraction than a
practical means of getting around, operate on
three routes between 6.30am and 12.30am:
Powell–Mason and Powell–Hyde run
between Market Street and Fisherman's Wharf,
and California Street runs between the
Financial District and Nob Hill. Tickets cost $6
per ride and can be bought from the self-
service machines at the end of each route, or
from the conductor when you board.

CAR RENTAL

● All international car-rental companies have
desks at SFO, as well as offices in the city.
● Alamo: SFO, tel 800/462–5266
● Avis: SFO, tel 800/230–4898
● Budget Rent-a-Car: SFO, tel 800/527–0700
● Dollar: SFO, tel 800/800–4000
● Dubbelju (motorcycles), tel 415/495–2774
● Hertz: SFO, tel 800/654–3131
● Seatbelts are compulsory for all passengers
and the driver. Child restraints are mandatory
for under six-year-olds or children weighing
less than 60lb (27kg).
● On-the-spot fines can be imposed for
speeding, with the level of fine depending on
the amount over the limit: over 25mph
(40kph), you may have to go to court.

TAXIS

Taxis can be hailed in the street or from taxi
stands at major hotels and at transportation
terminals. During rush hours (7–9am and
4–6pm) and rain, it is hard to find a free taxi
cruising the streets. Average taxi fares are
$3.10 for pick up and 45¢ per every fifth of a
mile. Hotel receptionists can order a taxi for
you on request, or you can phone one of the
following firms:
● De Soto, tel 415/970–1300
● Fog City, tel 415/285–8749
● Luxor, tel 415/282–4141
● Yellow, tel 415/333–3333

PARKING

Parking restrictions are
enforced with vigor. The city
has many off-street and
multistory parking lots, in
addition to meters, many of
which now take credit cards.
When parking on the city's
steep hills, you are required
by law to turn downhill-
facing vehicles' front wheels
into the curb; uphill-facing
vehicles should have their
wheels turned to the street.

CITY PASS

San Francisco offers visitors
the City Pass, which is a
booklet of tickets for sights in
the city. It costs $84 ($59 for
kids) and includes admission
for six attractions and a
seven-day MUNI and Cable
Car Passport. Sights include
Aquarium of the Bay, the
California Academy of
Sciences and the
Exploratorium.

Essential Facts

MONEY MATTERS

Nearly all banks have Automatic Teller Machines (ATMs). Credit cards are widely accepted. A 9.5 percent sales tax is added to marked retail prices. Funds can be wired via: American Express MoneyGram ☎ 800/926–9400 for US and Canada locations; Western Union ☎ 800/325–6000 for agent locations (or to send using MasterCard or Visa).

EMBASSIES

● Germany ✉ 1960 Jackson Street ☎ 415/775–1061
● Ireland ✉ 100 Pine Street ☎ 415/392–4214
● Italy ✉ 2590 Webster Street ☎ 415/292–9200
● Japan ✉ 50 Fremont Street ☎ 415/777–3533
● Mexico ✉ 532 Folsom Street ☎ 415/354–1700
● Spain ✉ 1405 Sutter Street ☎ 415/922–2995
● UK ✉ 1 Sansome Street, Suite 850 ☎ 415/617–1300

CURRENCY

The unit of currency is the dollar (=100 cents). Notes (bills) come in denominations of $1, $5, $10, $20, $50 and $100; coins are 25¢ (a quarter), 10¢ (a dime), 5¢ (a nickel) and 1¢ (a penny).

ELECTRICITY

The supply is 100 volts, 60 cycles AC current. US appliances use two-prong plugs. European appliances require an adapter.

EMERGENCY PHONE NUMBERS

● Fire, police or ambulance: 911
● Rape Crisis Hotline: 415/647–7273
● Victims of Crime Resource Center: 800/842–8467

LAVATORIES

Public buildings are obliged to provide lavatories, which are almost always well maintained, as are those in hotel lobbies, restaurants and most bars.

LOST PROPERTY PHONE NUMBERS

● San Francisco International Airport: 650/821–7014
● Amtrak station in Oakland: 800/872–7245
● MUNI buses or cable cars: 311

MEDICINES

Pharmacies are plentiful and details can be found online or in the Yellow Pages listed under "Drugstores." Visitors from Europe will find many familiar medicines sold under unfamiliar names. Note that some medication bought over the counter at home might be prescription-only in the US and may be confiscated at customs if you don't have a doctor's certificate for essential medication.

NEWSPAPERS AND MAGAZINES

San Francisco has two daily newspapers, the *San Francisco Chronicle* and the free *San Francisco Examiner*, and two free weekly papers, *SF Weekly* and *San Francisco Bay*

Guardian. Free tourist-aimed magazines are found in hotel lobbies; their discount coupons can save money on sightseeing and food.

OPENING HOURS
● Stores open daily, usually from around 10–6. Department stores, chain stores and shopping malls often have longer hours, while boutiques sometimes close on Sundays.
● Banks open Mon–Fri 9–4, 5 or 6; some branches open Saturday.
● Post offices usually open Mon–Fri 9–5.30, with limited hours on Saturday.

PLACES OF WORSHIP
Hotel receptions can advise and the phone book carries a comprehensive list.

POST SERVICES
● Stamps are available from post offices and also at some hotel receptions, vending machines and ATMs.
● Find the nearest post office by looking in the phone book or online or asking at your hotel.

PUBLIC HOLIDAYS
● Jan 1: New Year's Day
● Third Mon in Jan: Martin Luther King Day
● Third Mon in Feb: President's Day
● Last Mon in May: Memorial Day
● Jul 4: Independence Day
● First Mon in Sep: Labor Day
● Second Mon in Oct: Columbus Day
● Nov 11: Veterans' Day
● Fourth Thu in Nov: Thanksgiving Day
● Dec 25: Christmas Day

SENSIBLE PRECAUTIONS
San Francisco is one of the country's safest cities and lone travelers, especially women, are not unusual. Unwelcome attention is not unknown, and areas such as the Tenderloin, parts of the Mission, Oakland, the Haight, Golden Gate Park, Western Addition and the outskirts of the city, may seem threatening

ETIQUETTE
● Be aware of the anti-smoking feeling that prevails in San Francisco. Smoking is illegal in bars, restaurants and nightclubs throughout California.
● Tip at least 15 percent in a restaurant; 15–20 percent of a taxi fare; $1 per bag to a porter.

MEDICAL TREATMENT
● Doctor referral: San Francisco Medical Society ☎ 415/561–0850
● Dentist: San Francisco Dental Society ☎ 415/928–7337
● City hospitals with 24-hour emergency rooms:
San Francisco General ✉ 1001 Potrero Avenue ☎ 415/206–8000;
Davies Medical Center ✉ Castro Street (at Duboce Street) ☎ 415/600–6000
● Medicines: 24-hour pharmacy Walgreens offers a service at:
✉ 3201 Divisadero Street ☎ 415/931–6417;
✉ 498 Castro Street ☎ 415/861–3136
● It is strongly recommended to take out comprehensive medical insurance before traveling.

● San Francisco Convention
& Visitor Bureau ✉ 900
Market Street, Hallidie Plaza,
CA ☎ 415/391–2000;
www.onlyinsanfrancisco.com
● Convention and Visitors
Bureaux:
Berkeley ✉ 2030 Addison
Street, #102, Berkeley, CA
94704 ☎ 510/549–7040;
www.visitberkeley.com
Oakland ✉ 463 11th Street,
Oakland CA 94607
☎ 510/839–9000;
www.visitoakland.org
San Jose ✉ 408 Almaden
Boulevard, CA 95110
☎ 800/726–5673;
www.sanjose.org
Santa Clara ✉ 1850
Warburton Avenue, Santa
Clara, CA 95054
☎ 800/272–6822;
www.santaclara.org
● Travel package including
Visitors Guide and state map
☎ 800/862–2543
● Public library ✉ 100
Larkin Street (at Grove
Street) ☎ 415/557–4400

after dark. Do not carry easily snatched bags
and cameras, or stuff your wallet into your
back pocket. Always keep your belongings
within sight and within reach. Keep valuables
in the hotel's safe and never carry more
cash than you need. If you plan to make an
insurance claim, report any item stolen to the
nearest police precinct as soon as possible.
It is unlikely that any stolen goods will be
recovered, but the police will fill out the forms
that your insurance company will need.

TELEPHONES

● Thanks to the popularity of cell phones,
public telephones are now difficult to find,
although they can still sometimes be found
in the street, hotel lobbies, restaurants and
public buildings.
● Many businesses have toll-free numbers,
prefixed 800, 866, 877 or 888, allowing the
public to phone them for free. First dial "1."
● Most US phones use touch-tone dialing;
each button issues a different electronic tone
as it is pressed, enabling the caller to access
extensions directly, following the instructions
given by a recorded voice.
● The area code for San Francisco is 415,
which should not be dialed if calling from
another 415 number. The code for Berkeley
and Oakland is 510, and San Jose is 408.
● To call the operator dial "0."
● Dial 311 to reach the San Francisco
customer service line. You can call 24 hours a
day with questions about government-related
services—or even to report a pothole.

TELEVISION AND RADIO

● Linked to national networks, the main San
Francisco TV channels are 2, KTVU (FOX); 3,
KNTV (NBC); 5, KPIX (CBS); 7, KGO (ABC);
and the public-run 9, KQED (PBS). These give
the usual range of programs plus local and
national news.
● San Francisco has some 80 radio stations.
Generally, the best talk and news shows are
on the AM waveband, while the best music
is on FM stations.

Films and Books

FILMS

Vertigo (1958): This Hitchcock masterpiece stars Jimmy Stewart as an acrophobic San Francisco detective and Kim Novak as the woman he becomes obsessed with. Locations include Lombard Street, the Legion of Honor and Nob Hill.

The Graduate (1967): The coming-of-age drama features Dustin Hoffman as a recent college graduate and Anne Bancroft as Mrs. Robinson, the sexy older woman who seduces him.

Bullitt (1968): Lieutenant Frank Bullitt (Steve McQueen) must protect a Chicago mob boss turned government witness, but Bullitt soon discovers he doesn't have all the facts. The car chase through San Francisco is famous.

Dirty Harry (1971): Inspector Harry Callahan (Clint Eastwood) must stop a lunatic from terrorizing San Francisco. Locations include 555 California Street, City Hall, Mission Dolores Park and Washington Square.

Escape from Alcatraz (1979): This movie, based on a true story, focuses on a group of convicts (including one played by Clint Eastwood) who try to escape from Alcatraz.

Mrs. Doubtfire (1993): Robin Williams disguises himself as a nanny to spend time with his children after an ugly divorce. His new employer/ex-wife lives at 2640 Steiner Street.

The Rock (1996): This Michael Bay thriller features Nicolas Cage and Sean Connery as the good guys trying to stop a crazy general from launching warheads into San Francisco.

The Game (1997): Michael Douglas is a financier who receives an unusual birthday gift from his brother (Sean Penn). Watch for 555 California, the Embarcadero and the Presidio.

The Pursuit of Happyness (2006): This is based on Chris Gardner's true story about a man (played by Will Smith) who loses everything, but fights for survival and success. It shows Candlestick Park and Golden Gate Park.

Milk (2008): Sean Penn stars as politician and gay-rights activist Harvey Milk, the first openly gay elected official in California. The film was shot in locations all over San Francisco.

BOOKS

● *The Maltese Falcon* by Dashiell Hammett (1930): Hammett's influential detective novel was adapted into one of the first movies of the film noir genre, with Humphrey Bogart as private investigator Sam Spade.

● *On the Road* by Jack Kerouac (1951): The bible of the Beat Generation, part of this semi-autobiographical road-trip novel takes place in San Francisco, which figured prominently in the Beat movement.

● *Tales of the City* by Armistead Maupin (1978): What started as a newspaper serial morphed into a series of books about the escapades of Mary Ann Singleton, a woman who moves to San Francisco from Ohio.

● *The Joy Luck Club* by Amy Tan (1989): Mothers and daughters from four Chinese-American immigrant families start a mahjong club and share their stories.

● *Daughter of Fortune* by Isabel Allende (1999): Part 2 of this Oprah Book Club selection takes the protagonist to the City by the Bay.

Index

The Automobile Association would like to thank the following photographers, companies and picture libraries for their assistance in the preparation of this book.

Abbreviations for the picture credits are as follows – (t) top; (b) bottom; (c) center; (l) left; (r) right; (AA) AA World Travel Library.

2i AA/C Sawyer; 2ii AA/C Sawyer; 2iii AA/C Sawyer; 2iv Chris Howes/Wild Places Photography / Alamy; 2v AA/C Sawyer; 3i Bill Helsel/Alamy; 3ii AA/C Sawyer; 3iii Courtesy of Mandarin Oriental, San Francisco; 3iv AA/C Sawyer; 4 AA/C Sawyer; 5 AA/C Sawyer; 6/7t AA/C Sawyer; 6/7ct AA/C Sawyer; 7ct Lee Foster/Alamy; 6cb Lee Foster/Alamy; 6cb Photodisc; 6/7b KeystoneUSA-ZUMA/Rex Features; 8tr AA/C Sawyer; 9tl Chris Howes/Wild Places Photography / Alamy; 8/9c AA/K Paterson; 9ct Travel Division Images/Alamy; 9cb Courtesy of Cobb's Comedy Club; 8/9b AA/C Sawyer; 10l AA/K Paterson; 10r AA/K Paterson; 11 AA/C Sawyer; 12 AA/K Paterson; 14l David R. Frazier Photolibrary, Inc./Alamy; 14/15t AA/C Sawyer; 14/15c AA/C Sawyer; 15 AA/C Sawyer; 16 Paul Vidler/Alamy; 17tl Paul Vidler/Alamy; 17cl AA/C Sawyer; 17r Photolibrary/Getty Images; 18l Courtesy of Tim Griffith/California Academy of Sciences; 18tr Courtesy of Tim Griffith/California Academy of Sciences; 19tl Courtesy of Tim Griffith/California Academy of Sciences; 18/19c Courtesy of Tim Griffith/California Academy of Sciences; 19tr Courtesy of Charles Delbeek/California Academy of Sciences; 19cr Courtesy of Tim Griffith/California Academy of Sciences; 20 Courtesy of Chinese Historical Society of America; 21c Courtesy of Chinese Historical Society of America; 21tl Courtesy of Chinese Historical Society of America; 21tr Courtesy of Chinese Historical Society of America; 21cr Courtesy of Chinese Historical Society of America; 22 AA/C Sawyer; 23tl AA/C Sawyer; 23d Miguel A. Munoz Pellicer/Alamy; 23r Frank Tozier/Alamy; 24 AA/C Sawyer; 25tl AA/K Paterson; 25tr Lee Foster/Alamy; 25c David R. Frazier Photolibrary, Inc./Alamy; 26 Courtesy of The Neptune Society of Northern California; 27tl AA/C Sawyer; 27cl Robert Holmes/Corbis; 27r Courtesy of The Neptune Society of Northern California; 28l Monica M. Davey/epa/Corbis; 28/9t Art on File/Corbis; 28/9c Art on File/Corbis; 29r Architec Tour/Alamy; 30 Courtesy of Fine Arts Museums of San Francisco; 31tl Courtesy of Fine Arts Museums of San Francisco; 31cl Courtesy of Fine Arts Museums of San Francisco; 31r Courtesy of Fine Arts Museums of San Francisco; 32l Courtesy of Amy Snyder/Exploratorium; 32/3t Courtesy of Amy Snyder/Exploratorium; 32/32c Courtesy of Nancy Rodger/Exploratorium; 33tr Courtesy of Lily Rodriguez/Exploratorium; 33cr Courtesy of Amy Snyder/Exploratorium; 34l AA/C Sawyer; 34tr AA/C Sawyer; 34tl AA/C Sawyer; 35tr AA/C Sawyer; 34/5c AA/C Sawyer; 35cr John Gilbey/Alamy; 36 AA/K Paterson; 36/7 AA/C Sawyer; 38 AA/C Sawyer; 39tl AA/C Sawyer; 39c AA/L K Stow; 40 AA/C Sawyer; 41tl AA/C Sawyer; 41cl AA/K Paterson; 41tr AA/C Sawyer; 41cr AA/C Sawyer; 42l Neil Setchfield/Alamy; 42/3t Neil Setchfield/Alamy; 42/3c Jon Arnold Images Ltd/Alamy; 43tr AA/K Paterson; 43cr AA/C Sawyer; 44 Stefano Politi Markovina/Alamy; 45tl AA/C Sawyer; 45c Hemis/Alamy; 46l AA/C Sawyer; 46/7t AA/C Sawyer; 46/7c AA/C Sawyer; 47tr AA/C Sawyer; 47cr AA/C Sawyer; 48t Courtesy of Steve Whittaker/Fine Arts Museums of San Francisco; 48c AA/C Sawyer; 49l Courtesy of Steve Whittaker/Fine Arts Museums of San Francisco; 49tr Courtesy of Steve Whittaker/Fine Arts Museums of San Francisco; 49cr Courtesy of Fine Arts Museums of San Francisco; 50l AA/K Paterson; 50/1 AA/K Paterson; 51tr dbimages/Alamy; 51cr dk/Alamy; 52 Courtesy of Tim Griffith/Oakland Museum of California; 53tl Courtesy of Oakland Museum of California; 53c Courtesy of Oakland Museum of California; 54l AA/K Paterson; 54r San Francisco/Alamy; 54l AA/K Paterson; 55tr Aerial Archives/Alamy; 55cr Dennis Hallinan/Alamy; 56l AA/C Sawyer; 56/7 Craig Lovell/Eagle Visions Photography/Alamy; 57tr Courtesy of Richard Barnes/San Francisco Musuem of Modern Art; 57cr Ryan K. McGinnis/Alamy; 58/9 AA/C Sawyer; 59 Neil Fraser/Alamy; 60l Courtesy of UC Berkeley; 60/1t Courtesy of Steve McConnell/UC Berkeley; 60/1c Courtesy of Steve McConnell/UC Berkeley; 61r Courtesy of Steve McConnell/UC Berkeley; 62l AA/C Sawyer; 62/3t AA/C Sawyer; 62/3c AA/C Sawyer; 63 AA/C Sawyer; 64 AA/C Sawyer; 66 Courtesy of Kaz Tsuruta/Asian Art Museum; 67l AA/C Sawyer; 67r AA/C Sawyer; 68 AA/C Sawyer; 69l David Sanger Photography/Alamy; 69r AA/C Sawyer; 70l AA/C Sawyer; 70r AA/C Sawyer; 71 AA/C Sawyer; 72l AA/C Sawyer; 72r AA/C Sawyer; 73l Nikreates/Alamy; 73r AA/C Sawyer; 75l Lee Foster/Alamy; 75r AA/K Paterson; 76 Ambient Images Inc./Alamy; 77 Chad Ehlers/Alamy; 78 AA/C Sawyer; 79l AA/C Sawyer; 79r AA/C Sawyer; 80 Chris Howes/Wild Places Photography/Alamy; 82tr Dave Pattison/Alamy; 82bl Rubens Abboud/Alamy; 83t AA/C Sawyer; 83c Courtesy of Cesar Rubio/The Walt Disney Family Museum; 83b Dennis MacDonald/Alamy; 86i Courtesy of Amy Snyder/Exploratorium; 86ii AA/C Sawyer; 86iii AA/C Sawyer; 86iv Courtesy of Steve Whittaker/Fine Arts Museums of San Francisco; 86v Dennis Hallinan/Alamy; 87 AA/C Sawyer; 88t AA/C Sawyer; 88b AA/C Sawyer; 89t AA/C Sawyer; 89r AA/C Sawyer; 92t AA/C Sawyer; 92c AA/C Sawyer; 92b AA/K Paterson; 94t AA/C Sawyer; 94b AA/C Sawyer; 95t AA/K Sawyer; 95b AA/C Sawyer; 98l AA/K Paterson; 98r AA/C Sawyer; 100t AA/C Sawyer; 100b AA/C Sawyer; 101t AA/C Sawyer; 101c AA/C Sawyer; 101b dbimages/Alamy; 104t AA/C Sawyer; 104c AA/C Sawyer; 104b AA/K Paterson; 106t AA/C Sawyer; 106b Courtesy of Fine Arts Museums of San Francisco; 107t AA/C Sawyer; 107b AA/C Sawyer; 110i Courtesy of Tim Griffith/California Academy of Sciences; 110ii Courtesy of The Neptune Society of Northern California; 110iii Courtesy of Fine Arts Museums of San Francisco; 110iv AA/C Sawyer; 111l AA/C Sawyer; 111r AA/C Sawyer; 112t Steve McConnell/UC Berkeley; 112b Courtesy of Oakland Museum of California; 113t Lee Foster/Alamy; 113l AA/C Sawyer; 116t Courtesy of Oakland Museum of California; 116b Steve McConnell/UC Berkeley; 117 Courtesy of Bonnie Azab Powell/UC Berkely; 118 AA/C Sawyer; 120/1t AA/C Sawyer; 120/1ct AA/C Sawyer; 121ct AA/C Sawyer; 120/1cb AA/C Sawyer; 121cb AA/C Sawyer; 120/1b AA/C Sawyer; 126 AA/C Sawyer; 127 AA/C Sawyer; 128 Bill Helsel/Alamy; 130/1t AA/C Sawyer; 130/1c Emmanuel Rondeau/Alamy; 131ct AA/Y Levy; 131cb AA/Mockford & Bonetti; 130/1b Arco Images GmbH/Alamy; 137 Werner Dieterich/Alamy; 138 AA/C Sawyer; 140t Photodisc; 140ct AA/C Sawyer; 140cb AA/C Sawyer; 140b AA/C Sawyer; 142 Photodisc; 145 Photodisc; 147l Photodisc; 147r AA/T Carter; 148l Photodisc; 148r AA/J Tims; 150 Courtesy of Mandarin Oriental, San Francisco; 152t AA/Mockford & Bonetti; 152ct AA/K Paterson; 152cb AA/M Bonnet; 152b AA/J Tims; 156 Courtesy of Mandarin Oriental, San Francisco; 158 Lee Foster/Alamy; 160 AA/C Sawyer

Every effort has been made to trace the copyright holders, and we apologise in advance for any accidental errors. We would be happy to apply the corrections in the following edition of this publication.

Published by AA Publishing, a trading name of AA Media Limited, whose registered office is Fanum House, Basing View, Basingstoke, Hampshire RG21 4EA. Registered number 06112600.

© AA Media Limited 2015
First published 1996
New edition 2015

WRITTEN BY Mick Sinclair
ADDITIONAL WRITING BY Julie Jares
UPDATED BY Jane Egginton
SERIES EDITOR Clare Ashton
COVER DESIGN Tracey Freestone, Nick Johnston
DESIGN WORK Tracey Freestone
IMAGE RETOUCHING AND REPRO Ian Little

Colour separation by AA Digital Department
Printed and bound by Leo Paper Products, China

A CIP catalogue record for this book is available from the British Library.

ISBN 978-0-7495-7662-2

We have tried to ensure accuracy in this guide, but things do change, so please let us know if you have any comments at travelguides@theAA.com.

A05237
Maps in this title produced from map data supplied by Global Mapping, Brackley, UK © Global Mapping/ITMB
Transport map © Communicarta Ltd, UK

Titles in the Series

- Amsterdam
- Barcelona
- Boston
- Budapest
- Dublin
- Florence
- Istanbul
- Las Vegas
- London
- Madrid
- New York
- Orlando
- Paris
- Rome
- San Francisco
- Singapore
- Venice